Little Ways
to
Little Sanctity

*Walk the Way of Christ with Littleness
and Simplicity...One Step at a Time*

DANIEL J. THOMPSON

Little Ways to Little Sanctity:
Walk the Way of Christ with Littleness and Simplicity...One Step at a Time
by Daniel J. Thompson, published by O'Shee Publishing, LLC.

The information provided within this book is for informational purposes only. There are no representations or warranties, express or implied, about the completeness, accuracy, reliability, suitability or availability with respect to the information in this book for any purpose.

For details regarding book orders, please visit **www.amazon.com, www.barnesandnoble.com** or email the author at **Osheepublishing@gmail.com**
To order Deed Bead strand(s) please visit **www.gooddeadbeads.com**

Imprimatur
In accordance with CIC 827, permission to publish has been granted on November 21, 2017, by the Most Reverend Mark S. Rivituso, Auxiliary Bishop, Archdiocese of St. Louis. Permission to publish is an indication that nothing contrary to Church teaching is contained in this work. It does not imply any endorsement of the opinions expressed in the publication; nor is any liability assumed by this permission.

All images used with permission or sought permission.

Permission granted for Divine Mercy Chaplet image (Chapter Bead One): "Used with permission of the Marian Fathers of the Immaculate Conception of the B.V.M."

Scripture citations are taken from the New American Bible:
United States Conference of Catholic Bishops
3211 4th Street, N.E., Washington, DC 20017-1194
November 11, 2002 Copyright (c) by United States Conference of Catholic Bishops
http://www.vatican.va/archive/ENG0839/_INDEX.HTM

Cover Illustration by Walter Leamy
Cover design by Jennifer Kelly
Book design by Jennifer Kelly

ISBN# 978-1-7327396-0-4

Dedicated to my wife, Rose,
and my children, Danny, Maddie, Kate and Annie.
I cherish the gift and blessing that you are in my life.
The love we share is a treasure.

ACKNOWLEDGMENT

One of the most enjoyable aspects of writing *Little Ways to Little Sanctity* was the conversations, the comments and the advice that friends and family shared along the way. I had input and assistance from many people who are so important in my life. I can't begin to thank them all, but I want to mention a few. I want to thank my brother-in-law, Mike Loynd (author of *All Things Irish*), for his advice, input and edits. Similarly, I greatly appreciate the review and comments from my friend Rick Effer. My college friend and roommate, Monsignor Tom Powers provided great theological insight and advice and the Foreword that he contributed to *Little Ways* was so very much appreciated and helped bring clarity to my words. My wife Rose and my four children, Danny, Maddie, Kate and Annie were such inspirations through my writing journey. They were amazing sounding boards offering advice and guidance all along the way. They always were patient with me and constructive when I needed to talk through a topic or in seeking advice on a component of the book. I am also thankful for my great friend Ed "Schmed" Phillips, with whom we frequently discuss our walk in life which for us is akin to the Road to Emmaus. With Schmed, I am fortunate to share weekly discussions in faith and friendship and his input and support were inspiring and motivating. My sister, Mary Thompson Jose, was an amazing source of fortitude and persistence as she never gave up on me. She kept pushing and prodding me along the way with constructive advice at every juncture. And lastly, my dad started it all for me, not only through being a role model whom I admired in the accomplishment of his book, *Blood Revenge*, as well as his annual Christmas stories, but more importantly as an amazing role model as a Father. He provided the first editorial review and he supported me along the way. I was not able to finish *Little Ways* prior to his passing, but his mark will be enduring.

A very special friend to my father during the last years of his life was Walter Leamy. Walter and my dad were deeply committed to sharing the message of Mary as partners in the Legion of Mary. Walter provided great support to my father towards the end of his life and I am very grateful for his beautiful painting of Christ which adorns the cover of *Little Ways to Little Sanctity*.

Lastly and importantly, I can't begin to thank my friend Jennifer Kelly, the proprietor of Kelly Creative, for her artistic and creative talents which she brought to this undertaking. Jennifer has a special talent and I am thankful to her for the design and compilation.

GOOD DEED BEADS

Throughout *Little Ways to Little Sanctity*, you will find references to and images of Deed Bead strands. Deed Beads serve as an ideal tool to offer a subtle prodding on each and every day to account for and keep track of your little ways to little sanctity. I am very thankful to the Hercules Family for the images of Deed Beads which they provided and which are found throughout the book. These are actual strands of Deed Beads, which the Hercules Family produce and you can order your personal strand by visiting their website at **www.gooddeedbeads.com.**

TABLE OF CONTENTS

FOREWORD 8

INTRODUCTION 10

THE LITTLE WAYS OF SAINT THÉRÈSE OF LISIEUX 12

TEN "LITTLE WAYS" 20

BEAD ONE   *Increase in Prayer* 28

BEAD TWO   *Turn Away from Temptation* 40

BEAD THREE   *Be Charitable* 50

BEAD FOUR   *Humble Yourself, Become Little* 58

BEAD FIVE   *Suffer with Him* 70

BEAD SIX   *Adore Christ* 84

BEAD SEVEN   *Let Mary be your Advocate* 94

BEAD EIGHT   *Seek the Treasury of the Church* 112

BEAD NINE   *Embrace the Sacraments* 126

BEAD TEN   *Be an Ambassador for Christ* 142

CONCLUSION 152

FOREWORD

The Second Vatican Council's Dogmatic Constitution on the Church, *Lumen Gentium*, states that "all the faithful of Christ are invited to strive for the holiness and perfection of their own proper state. Indeed they have an obligation to so strive" (*LG* 42). That is to say that the call to holiness is not restricted to those in holy orders or consecrated religious; rather, there is, as the title of the document's fifth chapter makes clear, a *universal* call to holiness. Regardless of one's vocation, social status, age or condition, all the faithful of Christ are called to holiness. Sanctity is for everyone, and, with the Lord's grace and mercy, each member of the Church can become a saint.

That may sound overwhelming to many Christians today, especially when they compare their lives of faith to those of the great saints in Heaven. Would I have the charity of a St. Maximilian Kolbe or a St. Gianna Beretta Molla and willingly offer my life so that another may live? Could I ever possess the courage of a St. John Vianney or St. Pio and stand up to the onslaught of the Evil One? Would I crumble under the spiritual darkness endured by St. Thérèse of Lisieux or St. Teresa of Calcutta? Could I ever have profound prayer experiences like St. Gemma Galgani?

There is no question that we, and rightly so, are edified and inspired by the saints and enjoy reading about the heroic moments of their lives. However, we can also forget that the saints whom we admire and want to emulate did not necessarily become saints in one public, notable and heroic moment. They did not seek holiness in great acts. They sought holiness every day in the small, hidden and sometimes mundane events of their lives.

We are called to holiness, but are not called necessarily to singular moments of heroic sanctity. If we wait for those moments, they may never come; or worse, we may not be prepared for them. We, too, are given the opportunity to grow in charity and follow God's holy will in the small, hidden and sometimes mundane events of our lives. It is precisely there where we find the raw material for sanctity and where we can make small, but generous, acts of love for God.

Dan Thompson's book, *Little Ways to Little Sanctity*, is a wonderful guide to living out the universal call to holiness. He does a masterful job of introducing – and in some cases, reintroducing – to us saints of various historical eras, walks of life and vocations, who show us what sanctity looks like and how it is lived out every day. Furthermore, Mr. Thompson, a classmate from the University of Notre Dame and a dear friend, provides us with practical, memorable and, most importantly, achievable steps that we can practice throughout each day. These are the same means to holiness laid out in *Lumen Gentium*: prayer, detachment from the passing things of this world, charity, humility, suffering with Jesus, adoration, reliance on the Blessed Virgin Mary, fidelity to the Church, grace through the sacraments and confessing Christ before others.

In his presentation of these ten "Little Ways," Mr. Thompson reminds us that we need only take small steps, with love, and that the Lord will bless our efforts and give us the grace we need to continue step-by-step on the road to holiness. Unlike the popular slogans of our culture, which tell us to shape our own future, to live as though we are in complete charge of our lives and to seek more power and independence, the author demonstrates that the path of surrendering to and trusting completely in the Lord – and not in our personal accomplishments – is the one that leads to joy and peace. Furthermore, he provides concrete questions to contemplate so that each reader can apply the "Little Ways" to his or her own life and not hide in generalities.

In my varied and blessed ministry as a priest – which includes parish, high school and seminary work, and even ten years of service to the Holy See – I have met countless men and women who have sought out a contemporary, practical and easy-to-read book that would help them grow in their faith and bring them closer to the Lord. I was always able to recommend two or three books that would need to be read together, but I was never able to reduce the list to a single book. Until now.

I am certain that readers of all backgrounds and states of life will benefit spiritually from *Little Ways to Little Sanctity*, which offers straightforward advice regarding how each one of us, weak and small though we are, can respond to God's call to holiness so that we may one day share in His glory.

Monsignor Thomas W. Powers
Vicar General
Diocese of Bridgeport, CT

In the name of the Father,

And of the Son,

And of the Holy Spirit...

INTRODUCTION

In the ways of our Creator, the word "Little" is a big word with deep meaning. As we will see in the ensuing pages, so much goodness can be found in littleness. Our Lord Himself is a model for all. He did not come to conquer sin and darkness by power and primacy. Rather, He came in littleness and humility. He was the son of a carpenter. He was born in an off-the-road town, Bethlehem, in a stable amongst farm animals. As an infant, with His parents, He fled to foreign lands and lived an unremarkable childhood. He grew into an adult in relative anonymity and embarked on a ministry founded on truth and simplicity. He carried no belongings and had no home to rest His weary body nor to lay His head. His one luxury was to be carried into town, yet this triumphant ride was fleeting and on the back of an ass. He welcomed any and all as His brother or sister all the while receiving rebuke and criticism from the elite. From those who preached piety and purity, He was mocked and ridiculed. Ultimately, He suffered a lonely, brutal death, the death of a criminal, though innocent. Yet, He was a king, The King. His rule is forever and we are His subjects.

We are called to walk in His shoes, as best we can. This is not easy and from our imperfection as man, it is not natural. Yet, this is His way; therefore, we must strive to make it our way. By His example, if we can think in small ways and act in littleness, we can achieve greatness! It is a journey, yet one in which we can find peace and love if we let go the ways of the world; if we keep our focus on Him and practice love, one little way at a time.

The Little Ways of Saint Thérèse of Lisieux

"I am the way and the truth and the life. No one comes to the Father except through me." [1] It is here that Jesus teaches us all that we need to know about how we are to find eternal rest and comfort in the house of our Creator. He is the way; we need to follow His living example. He is the truth; we need to listen to and hear His Word. He is the life; we need to allow Christ to illuminate the path to everlasting salvation by modeling our life according to Jesus' humility and love. A simple message for sure, but a tall order to accomplish.

Saint Thérèse of Lisieux understood that the order of Christ was tall and, in her opinion, beyond the reach of a young, simple child. Thérèse was born January 2, 1873, in Alencon, France. She was one child of nine born to devoted parents who lost four of these children in their infancy and who offered the remaining five girls to a vocation in Christ upon their age of reason. In Thérèse's case, this gateway was opened to her at the early age of 15 in the cloister of the Carmel of Lisieux. This door did not open easily for Thérèse as she endured a childhood of pain and loss all the while her heart kept beating for her future spouse, the Heavenly King.

Thérèse's early childhood, however, in the region of Normandy, France was filled with the love of family and God. Her family was committed to the Word of God and they patiently practiced their faith through loving familial interactions, through their commitment to the daily celebration of the Mass, and their prayerful household. Thérèse enjoyed her rearing under the eyes of her parents who practiced the fine art of humility and love. Thérèse writes of fond family memories and a childhood swaddled in the love of her doting parents as described in her masterful lifelong memoir entitled *Story of a Soul*. Thérèse describes this comforting time in her life, "how quickly they passed by, those sunny years of my early childhood, but what a sweet imprint they left on my soul!" [2] "Everything on earth was smiling at me: I found flowers under every one of my steps, and my happy character also contributed to making my life pleasant." [3]

---

[1] John 14:6

[2] St. Thérèse of Lisieux. The Story of a Soul: A New Translation, translated by Robert J. Edmonson, CJ, (Paraclete Press, Brewster, Massachusetts) 2006, pg.22.

At the early age of five, Thérèse's blossoming childhood changed as quickly as the seasons can bring the chill of winter. Zelie Martin, Thérèse's mother, was diagnosed with breast cancer in 1876, and later succumbed to her cancer at the tender age of 46. At the passing of her mother, Thérèse remained deeply affected over the next nine years of her life which she describes as fraught with tears and sensitiveness. She came to rely heavily on the love of her sisters as a replacement for the hole left by her mother's loss. In particular, Thérèse grew lovingly fond of her older sister, Pauline.

Under the loving tutelage of the matriarch Pauline, the Martin sisters nurtured Thérèse through these tumultuous years. At times, she would live with her relatives only to return home to her Father and sisters where she felt most comforted and loved. Thérèse was emotional in all that she did, quick to tears and frequent outbursts, but her Father and siblings still nurtured her with the loving support that she needed. Thérèse described how fragile she was: "Oh! If God hadn't lavished His kindly rays on His little flower, she would never have been able to become acclimated to the earth. She was still too weak to endure rain and storms; she needed warmth, gentle dew and springtime breezes." [4] Life remained gloomy and devoid of true peace and joy until the season of Christmas some years later. In fact, it was Christmas Eve, December 24, 1886 when Thérèse found her way. On this fateful night, Thérèse explains, she received the gift of a special grace. At the age of 13, Thérèse felt the kiss of Christ and, in an instant, was given the gift of seeing how she would share her life henceforth, with her bridegroom, the Heavenly Host. She soon came to see her place in life to be as a humble, suffering servant at the foot of our Lord, and "so it is in the world of souls, which is Jesus' garden. He wanted to create great saints who could be compared to lilies and roses. But He also created little ones, and these ought to be content to be daisies or violets destined to gladden God's eyes when He glances down at His feet." [5]

Thérèse soon informed her Father of her intention to betroth herself to Jesus even at the young age of 15. She sought acceptance from the local Bishop who did not give his approval, but encouraged her to make a pilgrimage to Rome

---

[3] St. Thérèse, The Story of a Soul: A New Translation, pg. 23.

[4] St. Thérèse, The Story of a Soul: A New Translation, pg. 27.

[5] St. Thérèse, The Story of a Soul: A New Translation, pg. 5.

and allow her faith to grow and mature. However, Thérèse remained undeterred and upon her pilgrimage to Rome and a meeting with Pope Leo XIII, she broke protocol and spoke to the Pope pleading for his approval to enter Carmel at age 15. Pope Leo instructed her to follow the guidance of the religious Superiors yet exclaimed that she "will enter if it is God's will."[6] The will of God was meant to be and the Superiors conceded and welcomed Thérèse to Carmel on April 9, 1888. It was here that she offered herself to Jesus, her Bridegroom, as His little flower.

At the Order of Carmel, Thérèse came to believe that she did not have the capacity for great things for her Heavenly Father, yet committed herself to practicing little virtues in love. Her vocation to Christ was love; love in all that she did, and all that she did was little and humble. As she described her Little Way, "it is the way of spiritual childhood, the way of trust and complete surrender, … to offer Our Lord the flowers of little sacrifices and win Him by our proofs of love."[7] In reflecting on her little gifts of glory to God, as described in her memoir written near her death, Thérèse believed that "my mission is soon to begin, to make others love God as I do, to teach others my 'little way.'"[8] Thérèse practiced her humility and grew in sanctity, hidden before the eyes of all her Superiors and peers. She offered sacrifices at every turn of her day, all for the greater glory of her Heavenly Spouse. For example, Thérèse would not lean back against the support of her chair as a sacrifice for her Beloved. She would hold back a reply if it only served to prove her truthfulness or if it could serve to elevate her stature in the eyes of another. She ate all the food she was provided without ever complaining about food she did not like. Additionally, it was to the Sister in the cloister with whom she most questioned her attractiveness as holy before her Lord, that Thérèse would most work and incline herself to practice joy and friendship as a sacrifice to our lord for she understood that it was "Jesus hidden in the depths of her soul, Jesus who makes attractive even what is most bitter."[9] Thérèse sought to bring holiness out of the ordinary in her life which she attended to with love and conviction for Christ. She remained diligent in her every act, in each in every day, to live the message of Christ: "Amen, amen, I say to

[6] St. Thérèse, The Story of a Soul: A New Translation, pg. 152.

[7] St. Thérèse of Lisieux. *The Story of a Soul: The Autobiography of the Little Flower.* (Tan Classics, Charlotte, North Carolina) 2010, pg. 174.

[8] St. Thérèse of Lisieux. *The Story of a Soul: The Autobiography of the Little Flower*, pg. 173-174.

[9] St. Thérèse of Lisieux. *The Story of a Soul: The Autobiography of the Little Flower* pg. 131.

you, unless the grain of wheat falls into the ground and dies, it remains just a grain of wheat; but if it dies, it produces much fruit." [10]

Thérèse later contracted tuberculosis and experienced her first lung hemorrhage on Good Friday, April 3, 1896. At this time, she had been writing her memoir, which was private and not to be released until after her death. Her Mother Superior, who was also her sister Pauline, commissioned her to tell her life's story. It was not until after her death at the early age of 28, that the glorious flowers she gave to Christ became manifested for all the world to see. It is in her manuscript that the world begins to see and understand her Little Way. This was a way of trust and surrender to her Lord. Thérèse's way, though little, was magnanimous in faith. As Pope Pius XI stated in April 1923, "We earnestly desire that all the faithful should study her in order to copy her, becoming children themselves; since otherwise they cannot, according to the words of the Master, arrive at the kingdom of heaven." [11] He was referring to Christ's repeated instructions on the least and the last: "Whoever humbles himself like this child, is the greatest in the kingdom of heaven" [12] and "Amen, I say to you, unless you turn and become like children, you will not enter into the kingdom of heaven". [13] Christ further instructed, "Amen, I say to you, whoever does not accept the kingdom of God like a child will not enter it." [14]

St. Thérèse often taught that the focus of her Little Way was founded upon the Old Testament: " 'Whoever is a little one, let him come to me,' (Proverbs 9:4)" [15] " 'For to him that is little, mercy will be shown,' (Wisdom 6:7)" [16] and "'As one whom a mother caresses, so will I comfort you; in Jerusalem you shall find your comfort.' (Isaiah 66:12-13)" [17]

---

[10] John 12:24

[11] St. Thérèse of Lisieux. *The Story of a Soul: The Autobiography of Saint Thérèse of Lisieux*, (ICS Publications, Washington, DC, 3rd Edition) 1996, pg. xii.

[12] Matthew 18:4

[13] Matthew 18:3

[14] Mark 10:15

[15] St. Thérèse of Lisieux. *The Story of a Soul: The Autobiography of Saint Thérèse of Lisieux*. Third Edition Translated from the Original Manuscripts by John Clarke (ICS Publications, Washington, DC, 3rd Edition) 2013, Introduction.

[16] St. Thérèse of Lisieux. *The Story of a Soul: The Autobiography of Saint Thérèse of Lisieux*. Third Edition Translated from the Original Manuscripts by John Clarke (ICS Publications, Washington, DC, 3rd Edition) 2013, Introduction.

[17] St. Thérèse of Lisieux. *The Story of a Soul: The Autobiography of Saint Thérèse of Lisieux*. Third Edition Translated from the Original Manuscripts by John Clarke (ICS Publications, Washington, DC, 3rd Edition) 2013, Introduction.

During the process of her beatification and canonization, Pope Benedict XV announced that "In spiritual childhood is the secret of sanctity for all the faithful of the Catholic world." [18]   He further went on to teach that "there is a call to all the faithful of every nation, no matter what their age, sex, or state of life, to enter wholeheartedly into the Little Way which led Sister Thérèse to the summit of heroic virtue. It is our desire that the secret sanctity of Sister Thérèse of the Child Jesus be revealed to all our children." [19]   Pope Pius XI canonized her a saint only 28 years after her death, and on October 19, 1997, Pope John Paul II proclaimed her the third woman Doctor of the Church.

Saint Thérèse of the Child Jesus is honored on her feast day, October 1, as Patroness of the Missions. As the 33rd Doctor of the Church, and the youngest Doctor, she is recognized not for her great scholarship of theology, but rather for her practice of virtue, and her life of love as described in the Gospels. A model and beloved saint by Catholic patrons the world over, she is often described as the greatest saint of modern times. On her deathbed, she proclaimed, "My mission… to make God loved...will begin after my death...I will spend my heaven doing good on earth. I will let fall a shower of roses." [20] Roses have been described and experienced as Saint Thérèse's signature for many who have sought and found her intercession. [21]

Shortly before her death on September 30, 1897, Thérèse stated that "I feel that my mission is about to begin, my mission of bringing others to love our God as I love Him, teaching souls my little way of trust and self-surrender." [22] As summarized in *Lives of the Saints* for her Feast Day of October 1, "Love of God as a Father, expressed in childlike simplicity and trust, and a deep understanding of the mystery of the cross, were the basic principles of her 'Little Way.'" [23]

[18] St. Thérèse of Lisieux. *The Story of a Soul: The Autobiography of Saint Thérèse of Lisieux*, pg. xii.

[19] St. Thérèse of Lisieux. *The Story of a Soul: The Autobiography of Saint Thérèse of Lisieux*, pg. xii.

[20] www.Littleflower.org

[21] http://www.dollsfromheaven.com/shower-of-roses-testimonials/shower-of-roses-testimonials

[22] Reverend Lawrence G Lovasik, S.V.D. *Pocket book of Catholic Novenas*, 1997.

[23] Reverend Thomas J Donaghy. *Lives of the Saints II* – June 1, 1993
by Catholic Book Publishing Co (Author), Reverend Thomas J Donaghy (Author)

Thérèse wanted to be a person of holiness and purity for her Lord, but believed she was both unworthy and incapable of achieving the requisite sanctity that Our Father wants for us. In her mind, she was too simple, too lowly. From such a being of smallness Thérèse wondered, how could one so simple attain the purity her Bridegroom sought? Yet, even misunderstanding her own worthiness before Our Lord, Thérèse lived in childlike purity, perpetual humility, and gentle love in each "little" moment of her life. Unbeknownst to her, and others, she walked the narrow road to Christ, step by step, growing in littleness, growing in sanctity.

Thérèse came to see that the way of becoming holy was through fidelity to Christ and to His love through little things. As she described her gifts to her heavenly Spouse, "So, my Beloved, shall my short life be spent in Your sight. I can prove my love only by scattering flowers, that is to say, by never letting slip a single little sacrifice, a single glance, a single word; by making profit of the very smallest of actions, by doing them for love." [24]

For a countless number of the faithful, Thérèse has become a model of sanctity achieved by an imperfect child of God who sought love in all she did and who practiced humility in every way. The least of these is a diminutive woman named Agnes Gonxha Bojaxhiu from Skopje, Macedonia. This lowly child of God is now recognized as the newly canonized Saint Mother Teresa of Calcutta. Saint Teresa of Calcutta took her vows in 1928 for the Sisters of Our Lady of Loreto and chose her namesake after Saint Thérèse of Lisieux. She spoke in ways that modeled those of Saint Thérèse: "To the good God, nothing is little because He is so great and we so small – that is why He stoops down and takes the trouble to make those little things for us – to give us a chance to prove our love for Him. Because He makes them, they are very great. He cannot make anything small; they are infinite. Yes my dear children, be faithful in little practices of love, of little sacrifices – of the little interior mortifications – of little fidelities to Rule, which will build in you the life of holiness – make you Christ-like." [25]

Saint Thérèse of Lisieux believed herself too small and too insignificant to achieve greatness in the call of Christ. Yet, she came to find comfort in the little deeds that she was capable of offering to her Savior. In this, she excelled. Without the knowledge of those around her, Thérèse routinely practiced love and humility for God by means of little acts. These Little Ways of Saint Thérèse have since become known by and practiced by many the world over. Saint Thérèse popularized the use of Deed Beads to count her Little Ways, and she used her beaded strand of 10 Deed Beads to count her little ways, to denote her daily sacrifices of love for her heavenly King. [26] This hidden strand in her apron pocket was but a tangible lifeline of her hidden ways to sanctity.

[24] St. Thérèse of Lisieux. *The Story of a Soul: The Autobiography of the Little Flower* pg. 165.

[25] Brian Kolodiejchuk. *Mother Teresa, Come Be My Light*, the private writings of the "Saint of Calcutta", Mother Teresa to the Mission of Charity Sisters first Friday, November 1960, 35.

[26] http://cathfamily.org/st-Thérèse-of-lisieux-living-faith-beads

Ten "Little Ways"

Good Deed Beads gained popularity in use following the sanctity achieved by Saint Thérèse. Thérèse used her beaded strand of 10 beads as stepping stones on the path to salvation. Saint Thérèse carried her Deed Beads in her pocket at all times, and used them throughout the day by sliding a bead along the strand each and every time that she acted in holiness, whether it be little or great. She demonstrated power and a sustained growth in holiness by her daily commitment to doing small acts to advance in sanctity, counting each and every act by moving a bead along the strand of her Deed Beads.

Beads have been an important instrument for many Catholics today and throughout history as they walk the way of Christ along the chain of their rosaries. Thus, beads are a common touchstone for Catholics who strive to walk the way of our Lord, step by step, bead by bead. Walking the road to Bethlehem becomes alive in the Joyful Mysteries of the rosary. Walking the Ministry of Christ brings to light the Luminous Mysteries. Walking the Road to Calvary along the Via Dolorosa ("Way of Sorrows", the road Christ walked on His way from the scourging to Calvary) is relived in each of the Sorrowful Mysteries. Walking the Road to Emmaus and to the Mount of Ascension brings the Glorious Mysteries to life. So too can the use of Deed Beads be brought to bear for a step-by-step approach, little by little, to a life in Christ. *Little Ways to Little Sanctity!*

By her example, Saint Thérèse taught us just how sanctifying her Little Ways can be. She showed the world that holiness can be attained by a sustained commitment to making the ordinary, extraordinary. Little step by little step. Such little acts of charity and love are commonly found in the Bible, exemplifying Christ's message of love, and the significance of which, though arguably small in act, are large in impact. Recall the woman's anointing of Christ's body at Simon's house in Bethany. As she purified Christ's head with her perfumed chrism, Christ spoke of her demonstrable gift of love, although for those in attendance at this dinner banquet, this was an oddity at best and viewed as an intrusion into the Rabbi's evening. However, Christ taught of the significance of her little act of love as something that future generations would forever recount, "Amen I say to you, wherever this gospel is proclaimed in the whole world, what she has done will be spoken of, in memory of her." [27]

So too did littleness bring forth a wondrous proclamation in the town of Samaria, where Jesus came to stop and rest at the local well where a woman was also. Jesus asked for a simple act of kindness, on his behalf, that she draw him up some water. Her reception to this opportunity for charity in an act of love, brought about a discourse of revelation to her that He was the Christ, the Savior for all the world. Here before this simple woman who offered Him refreshing water from the well, Christ proclaimed that from Him came forth the everlasting water for all the world as He was the Messiah. Rejuvenated by His message, she sought all her townspeople to draw them in as well to this beautiful mystery that was now at hand. "Many of the Samaritans of that town began to believe in him because of the word of the woman who testified." [28] They confided to her that "We no longer believe because of your word; for we have heard for ourselves, and we know that this is truly the savior of the world." [29] The impact of her simple openness to Christ's request for a simple act of love brought great salvation to all the townspeople.

---

[27] Matthew 26:13

[28] John 4:39

[29] John 4:42

Again, Christ's gift of salvation was open to all who showed him kindness and mercy. As Jesus hung at the gibbet, taking upon Himself the sins of all the world and reconciling mankind to God, He opened His kingdom to the "good thief" who publicly defended Christ's name before all his executioners. It is on the cross, just before Christ expels his last, that Luke introduces the world to the "good thief" who openly defends our Lord before the gallery. "We have been condemned justly, for the sentence we received corresponds to our crimes, but this man has done nothing criminal." He then asked Jesus to remember him when He comes into His kingdom. Jesus rewards his act of humility, "Amen, I say to you, today you will be with me in Paradise." [30] Eternal salvation became the gift to the man who hung next to Christ, to the thief who truthfully and openly proclaimed the innocence of the Son of Man.

We are also introduced to the gifts and blessings that await each of us that act in faith. The man we have learned of who was a centurion that led a garrison of soldiers in the city of Capernaum, came before our Lord in faith. He was not of the House of David, yet possessed a confidence in Christ, a faith in He who came to lead. This was a simple and pure faith not found in many who proclaimed their piety. For this centurion sought Christ's healing for his suffering and paralyzed servant. Although the servant was not present, the centurion had unquestioning belief in the power that Jesus could command. The centurion replied to Jesus' offer to visit his servant, "Lord, I am not worthy to have you come under my roof; only say the word and my servant will be healed. For I too am a person subject to authority, with soldiers subject to me. And I say to one, 'Go,' and he goes; and to another, 'Come here', and he comes; and to my slave, 'Do this,' and he does it." [31] Jesus rewarded this honorable man's simple act of faith: "'Amen, I say to you, in no one in Israel have I found such faith.' ...And Jesus said to the centurion, "'You may go; as you have believed, let it be done for you.' And at that very hour (his) servant was healed." [32]

Similarly, a woman plagued with persistent hemorrhage, sought and found the healing of Jesus through her simple act of faith. As the rabbi walked by amongst

---

[30] Luke 23:41-43

[31] Matthew 8:8-9

[32] Matthew 8:10-13

[33] Mark 5:28

a throng of followers, the woman reached out and touched His cloak for she believed "If I just touch his clothes, I shall be cured." [33] Jesus questioned her actions and let all hear of the faith she professed. Jesus rewarded her simple and little act of faith, "Daughter, your faith has saved you. Go in peace and be cured of your affliction." [34]

The gift of salvation can similarly be found in a simple "thank you." In Luke's Gospel, Jesus cured 10 lepers while on a journey to Jerusalem. He instructed the 10 lepers to go show themselves to the local priest, and on their way, they were cleansed of their leprosy. Nine continued on their way, yet one of the ten felt compelled to humble himself before our Lord in gratitude. He returned to Jesus giving him glory and thanks. Jesus replied, "Ten were cleansed, were they not? Where are the other nine? Has none but this foreigner returned to give thanks to God?" [35] Jesus, accepting the man's simple act of gratitude and humility, granted him eternal salvation. "Stand up and go; your faith has saved you." [36]

Jesus came to call the lowly, the poor of heart, the lost sheep, the humble servant. He came to call all of us who are found in the lowly, the poverty stricken, the lost and the humble. It is us that Christ sought 2000 years ago, and it us who Christ is seeking today. While standing upon the Mount, Jesus offered a Sermon with bold new ideas brought down from His Heavenly Father, "Blessed are the poor in spirit, for theirs is the kingdom of heaven." [37] The meek will inherit the land, and the merciful will be shown Christ's mercy. "Blessed are the clean of heart, for they shall see God." [38] Jesus was and is asking for us, for you and for me. His gift is before us, we need merely to reach out for him in our thoughts and in our actions. Little steps on the narrow path is all that Christ is asking. He asks us to be simple and childlike. He asks us to act with an intention of purity and love, for Him. Jesus proclaims that salvation is at hand for those who seek him in simplicity, "I give you praise, Father, Lord of heaven and earth, for although you have hidden these things from the wise and the learned you have revealed them to the childlike." [39]

---

[34] Mark 5:34

[35] Luke 17:17-18

[36] Luke 17:19

[37] Matthew 5:3

[38] Matthew 5:8

[39] Matthew 11:25

Thus, the way, the truth and the life is found in littleness. It is in childlike humility that we will come to know and love Christ more fully. As Saint Thérèse found sanctity in her "little ways", so too can we begin to grow in sanctity, little sanctity, as we begin to practice her "little ways". Just as many of us may recall in the decades old commercial for Tootsie Pop lollipops, the gift inside was most sweetly achieved by a 1000 little licks of the pop. Nothing in the dramatic, nothing in the abrupt, but slow and steady brought forth the eternal goodness. Similarly, little ways were Saint Thérèse's life saver, earning her eternal life. Thérèse's life was profound in that she revealed to all the world, the little ways she practiced for a slow and steady walk to Christ.

Author Don Osgood made a random acquaintance while on a train excursion across the US. This acquaintance penned a personal prayer written during a period of distress in her life that illuminates the place we occupy in God's Kingdom when we become childlike: "The wind is the breath of God. The sun is the smile of God. The stars are the eyes of God. The rain is the tears of God. And children are the heart of God." [40]

Just as little sins can draw us in to bigger sins, making the misstep all the more easy with sinful practice. So too, Christ proclaimed and Thérèse understood, that little sanctity could be achieved through little acts of love for Him. Little steps along the walk of life will make the ordinary, extraordinary. References herein to "little" sanctity are not intended to diminish in any way the profound beauty of sanctity, of holiness. This is God's call for every one of us and it is truly great.

With our "deed beads" in tow, whether in purse or pocket, we can practice consistent humility and love for our Lord. Just as Jesus brought sustenance for those who hungered when he multiplied the fish and the loaves, so too can we multiply Christ's blessings by consistent and persistent acts of littleness, kindness, faith, charity, humility, obedience, and love. We can nourish the lives of others and walk the way to sanctity by participating in the multiplication of God's gifts to us through the practice of implementing little ways in our daily life. We can use our deed beads to count the ways.

Our Father in Heaven has graced us each with different gifts, that in a way, He has cast to the winds and is watching to see what we do with what we have received.

Some are tall and some are small. Some are rich and have things of plenty; others are impoverished and are continually in want. Some have beauty and others may be lacking. Yet, we each have a heart by which to love and we each have an internal free will by which we can choose. Our lot in life however, remains complicated by our natural inclination towards sin. This, our concupiscence, or our proclivity towards sin, is a path we will likely follow if we don't utilize our heart to love and our free will to choose otherwise. Consider a toll road which we each have traveled along during a journey in our life. Here we find ourselves with the path set forth before us to take us where we want to go. It may be long and it may be arduous. Along the way we need to pay tolls to continue on this path. However, the tolls we remit can be applied for the good of many by keeping the roadway clean, safe, and intact to enable a fruitful journey. So too are our lives similar to the toll road. We are all on a journey seeking the home of our Heavenly Father. The path is set forth before us and we can choose the way that is pure, safe, and leads to a fruitful journey and a celebratory conclusion. On this journey, we must pay tolls to remain upon the path of righteousness, to follow His Way. These tolls are the many times we are called to faith, or offered opportunity for charity, love, and kindness, or moments to sacrifice for Him. Think of each of these little ways, these inconsequential opportunities, as tolls we can offer for Him, that contribute back to our journey by keeping us on the right path, a path that remains fruitful. Each little toll can reorient us to the path we need to follow. It gives to Jesus who is asking for us and who is seeking from us. Each little toll is an investment back into our journey of life. Remember, the Father has clearly communicated that we will be asked to account for our actions and to he that has been given much, much will be expected in return. [41]

So take the beaded strand of 10 deed beads and feel them routinely throughout your day as they fumble in your pocket. Use your deed beads to walk the way of Christ along your 10 simple, little beads. During your day, find a way to be poor in spirit, to be meek and merciful, or pure of heart, for littleness will bring you nearer to Christ. Every time you successfully accomplish a "little way," move a bead along your deed bead strand. Seek not the ignorance of the wise and the learned, or the comforts of the rich and the selfish. Become little like a child, a

[40] Don Osgood *Listening for God's Silent Language*, 1995, 198.

[41] Luke 12:48

child in Christ by practicing Thérèse's little ways throughout your day. Whether you are successful in moving all ten beads or only one, each day is a journey in love for your neighbor, for yourself and most importantly for your Creator. In our human relationships whether with spouse, parent, friend or foe, each day brings new opportunities to attune ourselves to the needs of another, to dedicate effort towards meeting the needs of another and advancing the relationship. So too, the opportunity exists to deepen our relationship with Christ through a daily commitment to reaching beyond our comfort zone and seeking ways to walk His way, to bring to life His truth, and to commit ourselves to His life.

Strive to find 10 little ways each day to grow in sanctity, little by little. Each time during your day that you find a way to offer a toll and to take a step closer to Christ through littleness, move one bead. If you sacrifice, move a bead. If you pray, move a bead. If you provide charity to a neighbor or read the bible, move a bead. Begin to take little steps along the path to salvation, practicing little ways for Christ. As Saint Mother Teresa so simply professed, "Love is proved by deeds, the more they cost us, the more they prove our love." [42]

The next ten chapters that follow offer ten different ways suggested by the author by which we can practice Thérèse's Little Ways, and ultimately, help us to grow in holiness.

Walk this way.

---

[42] Edward Le Joly, S.J. *Mother Teresa of Calcutta: A Biography*, 1983, 179.

You are but the brush in the hand of the artist, nothing more. Tell me, what is a brush good for if it doesn't let the artist do his work? [43]

BEAD ONE

Increase in Prayer

Move a deed bead every time during your day that you find time to reach out to our Lord in prayer. Prayer can be a profound moment of time where you kneel in quiet contemplation and discourse with our Lord. Alternatively, prayer can be a moment in time during your busy day, where you stop to acknowledge the greatness of our God. Either of these is a reflection in time of you to our Creator and can be your gift to God. As Saint Thérèse described, "For me, prayer is a surge of the heart; it is a simple look turned toward heaven, it is a cry of recognition and of love, embracing both trial and joy." [44] However, Saint John Damascene challenges us in prayer, "when we pray, do we speak from the height of our pride and will, or out of the depths of a humble and contrite heart?" [45] Thus, in prayer, strive to be humble and seek the will of God for "the one who humbles himself will be exalted." [46]

As Saint Josemaria Escriva described, we need to let God our Creator, the Artist, do His work. Seek time during your busy day to step away and find the face of God. Reach out to Him in simple prayer or deep contemplation, but make the time. Jesus will hear and embrace your prayer. For as Christ taught, "all that you ask for in prayer, believe that you will receive it and it shall be yours." [47] Jesus taught his disciples to seek the Father in prayer, seek the Son, and seek the Holy Spirit. Embrace God in prayer with a filial love and trust that His will shall be

---

[43] St. JoseMaria Escriva. *The Way, Furrow, the Forge*, (Scepter Publishing, New York, New York) 1988, the Way verse 612, pg. 151.

[44] *Catechism of the Catholic Church: Revised in Accordance with the Official Latin Text Promulgated by Pope John Paul II.* 2nd ed. [Vatican City]: Libreria Editrice Vaticana, 2007, §2559, pg 613 as St. Thérèse of Lisieux. *Manuscripts autobiographiques*, C 25r.

[45] *CCC 2559*, pg 613 as St. John Damascene, *De fide* orth. 3, 24: Pg 94, 1089C.

[46] Luke 18:14

[47] Mark 11:24

done. "Knock and the door will be opened to you," [48] for "how much more will the Father in heaven give the Holy Spirit to those who ask him?" [49]

Prayer was certainly an active and important part of Christ's life. He routinely sought His Father in prayer and was a model to all in this regard. Following His baptism, Jesus prayed and heaven was opened and the Holy Spirit descended upon Him and the Father proclaimed, "You are my beloved Son; with you I am well pleased." [50] Although the throng of people would seek Him and follow Him, and He would minister to them with miraculous healings or profound teaching, He would still "withdraw to deserted places to pray" [51] or move off "to the mountain to pray". [52] Jesus even invited the companionship of His trusted apostles during His agonizing prayer to His Father while in the Garden of Gethsemane as His impending arrest drew near. [53] Prayer was indeed an active and integral part of Christ's relationship with His Father even up to His final breath.

Christ even prayed to His Father while suffering upon the Cross. Here during His heightened state of agony on behalf of mankind, our Lord still sought His Father in prayer. That is, Jesus' cry to His Heavenly Father, "My God, my God, why have you forsaken me?" [54], was a recitation of the prayer known by all Jews at the time as Psalm 22 of the Old Testament. "The Prayer of the Innocent Man", begins with these very words, "My God, my God, why have you forsaken me?" Psalm 22 goes on to further describe the suffering, brutality, and crucifixion at the hands of His enemies, while the Psalm evolves into a proclamation of glory for the Creator, "For He has not spurned or disdained the misery of this poor wretch, did not turn away from me, but heard me when I cried out." [55] The concluding glory was known by all Jews, in this often proclaimed Psalm, "The generation to come will be told of the Lord, that they may proclaim to a people yet unborn the deliverance you have brought." [56] Christ's cry to His Father in prayer was heard and answered for the salvation of all.

---

[48] Luke 11:9

[49] Luke 11:13

[50] Luke 3:21-22

[51] Luke 5:16

[52] Luke 6:12

[53] Matthew 26:36-41

We must not only seek the Father in prayer during times when we are in most need. We must also learn to seek Christ during the simple moments of our day, of our life. "Prayer in the events of each day and each moment is one of the secrets of the kingdom revealed to 'little children'".[57] As St. John Chrysostom proclaimed, "It is possible to offer fervent prayer even while walking in public or strolling alone, or seated in your shop, …while buying or selling, …or even while cooking."[58] Similarly, St. Paul instructed both the Ephesians and the Thessalonians to "Rejoice always. Pray without ceasing."[59], "giving thanks always and for everything in the name of our Lord Jesus Christ to God the Father."[60]

Thus, with deed beads in tow, find time and ways during your day to reach out to our Lord in prayer. Pray for gifts and graces. Pray for mercy or relief from temptation. Pray for reconciliation or strength. As St Thérèse describes, "prayer in my opinion is nothing else than a close sharing between friends; it means taking time frequently to be alone with him who we know loves us."[61]

With your deed beads, pray for deceased sinners as their hours on earth, to reconcile themselves before our Lord, have come and gone. A great prayerful gift that you can give to those in Purgatory was taught to St. Gertrude the Great around the close of the 13th Century. Our Lord told St. Gertrude that the following prayer would release 1000 souls from Purgatory each time it is said:

"Eternal Father, I offer thee the most precious blood of thy Divine Son,
Jesus, in union with the Masses said throughout the world today,
for all the Holy Souls in Purgatory, for sinners everywhere,
for sinners in the universal church,
those in my own home and within my family. Amen."[62]

---

[54] Matthew 27:46

[55] Psalm 22:25

[56] Psalm 22:32

[57] *CCC* 2660, pg. 639.

[58] *CCC* 2743, pg. 658 as St. John Chrysostom. Ecloga de oration 2:PG 63, 585.

[59] 1 Thessalonians 5:16-17

[60] Ephesians 5:20

[61] *CCC* 2709, pg. 650 as St. Teresa of Jesus. *The Book of Her Life*, 8, 5.

[62] http://www.catholictradition.org/Gertrude/saint-gertrude7.htm

This prayer is a beautiful and humble offering of Christ, sacrificed in the daily Mass, for the glory of God. I developed a personal challenge which was to pray St. Gertrude's prayer steadily and persistently for the release of more than three million souls from Purgatory and for their heavenly bliss with our Savior. Prayerfully, I have met and exceeded my personal challenge and I often seek the intercession of this three million strong, and growing, contingent of heavenly souls. On occasion, I seek the assistance of these millions of souls to come before the Heavenly Host with prayers on my behalf, for assistance in my prayerful needs. I lovingly look forward to the day when I will get to greet all of these heavenly souls whom my prayers have aided. I believe we now share a bond of love and commitment in Christ and I trust in their delight at our momentous meeting. By diligent recitation of St. Gertrude's prayer, challenge yourself to bring merciful assistance and the heavenly reward of eternal salvation to a throng of souls in Purgatory.

With your deed beads, pray for your enemies or for those with whom you struggle to find joy and happiness within your daily interactions. As Jesus taught in His Sermon on the Mount, "love your enemies, and pray for those who persecute you, that you may be children of your heavenly Father, for he makes his sun rise on the bad and the good, and causes rain to fall on the just and the unjust." [63] In childlike humility, want goodness and graces for those that are your enemies. Give prayerful love to those for whom you have disdain. As Jesus explained so simply, it is easy to love those close to us, but it takes true love to reach out to those for whom our love is lacking. "For if you love those who love you, what recompense will you have? Do not the tax collectors do the same?" [64] Jesus goes on to tell us to "be perfect, just as your heavenly Father is perfect." [65] This may seem to most like a tall order, impossible to attain. Correct you are, it is impossible for man to be perfect, but all is possible with the brush in the hand of the Heavenly artist, our Creator. "For human beings this is impossible, but for God all things are possible." [66] So trust in our Lord, and seek him in all that you do, reach out to him in prayer throughout your day.

---

[63] Matthew 5:43-45

[64] Matthew 5:46

[65] Matthew 5:48

[66] Matthew 19:26

[67] Luke 10:29

Converse with our Lord with simplicity and routineness, just as you would a friend or neighbor. Our neighbor can be an expected friend or can be found in the unexpectedness of a stranger. "Who is my neighbor?" [67] asked the scholar of the law as he sought to test the Master. Jesus went on to tell the "Parable of the Good Samaritan" and concluded by asking, "Which of these three, in your opinion, was neighbor to the robber's victim?" Jesus proclaimed for all the world to hear, that it was "the one who treated him with mercy...go and do likewise." [68] So make a connection to friend or foe by a prayerful plea to your Heavenly Father.

Pray the Rosary, all four Mysteries, one Mystery, or one decade. Be determined in your efforts to routinely draw the beads of the Rosary through your fingers. The beauty in the Rosary lies in the walk in faith you undergo as you circle your beautiful chain. Whether it be the Joyful Mysteries, the Luminous Mysteries, the Sorrowful Mysteries, or the Glorious Mysteries, with each you live the life of Christ and traverse the Gospels. The Blessed Virgin Mary spoke to St. Dominic and Blessed Alan and proclaimed the wonderful graces found in the recitation of the Rosary:

- Whoever shall faithfully serve me by the recitation of the Rosary, shall receive signal graces
- I promise my special protection and the greatest graces to all those who shall recite the Rosary
- The Rosary shall be a powerful armor against hell, it will destroy vice, decrease sin, and defeat heresies
- It will cause virtue and good works to flourish; it will obtain for souls the abundant mercy of God; it will withdraw the hearts of men from the love of the world and its vanities, and will lift them to the desire of eternal things. Oh, that souls would sanctify themselves by this means
- The soul which recommends itself to me by the recitation of the Rosary, shall not perish
- Whoever shall recite the Rosary devoutly, applying himself to the consideration of its sacred mysteries shall never be conquered by misfortune. God will not chastise him in His justice, he shall not perish by an unprovided death; if he be just he shall remain in the grace of God, and become worthy of eternal life

---

[68] Luke 10:29-37

- Whoever shall have a true devotion to the Rosary shall not die without the sacraments of the Church
- Those who are faithful to recite the Rosary shall have during their life and at their death the light of God and the plentitude of His graces; at the moment of death they shall participate in the merits of the saints in paradise
- I shall deliver from purgatory those who have been devoted to the Rosary
- The faithful children of the Rosary shall merit a high degree of glory in heaven
- You shall obtain all you ask of me by the recitation of the Rosary
- All those who propagate the holy Rosary shall be aided by me in their necessities
- I have obtained from my Divine Son that all the advocates of the Rosary shall have for intercessors the entire celestial court during their life and at the hour of their death
- All who recite the Rosary are my sons, and brothers of my only Son Jesus Christ
- Devotion of my Rosary is a great sign of predestination [69]

Another way to increase your time in prayer is by finding time during your day to read the Bible and allow this to be a means of prayer between you and your Father. The Catechism of the Catholic Church teaches "And such is the force and power of the Word of God that it can serve the Church as her support and vigor and the children of the Church as strength for their faith, food for the soul, and a pure and lasting font of spiritual life." [70] The Church further exhorts "all the Christian faithful…to learn the surpassing knowledge of Jesus Christ, by frequent reading of the divine Scriptures. Ignorance of the Scriptures is ignorance of Christ." [71] Draw a bead along as you sing a psalm, read a proverb, or walk the life of Christ through the pages of the Gospel. Time in the Bible is not the issue, it is your commitment and consistency to drawing in the Word of God on a daily and routine basis.

Come to know the beauty of the Divine Mercy Chaplet. Rapidly becoming one of the most important feast days of the year, Divine Mercy Sunday occurs on the

---

[69] https://www.ourladyswarriors.org/prayer/15promise.htm

[70] *CCC* 131, pg. 37 as *Dei Verbum* 21.

[71] *CCC* 133, pg. 37 as *Dei Verbum* 25; cf Phil 3:8 and St. Jerome, *Commentariorum in Isaiam libri xviii prol.*: J.P. Migne, ed., Patrologia Graeca (Paris, 1841-1855).

first Sunday after Easter. Saint Maria Faustina Kowalska was the recipient of Jesus' grace and guidance during the last 4 years of her life when He taught her lessons of His unfathomable mercy. Jesus taught this simple nun that He was the portal to eternal salvation and that all who sought Him with love and a plea for forgiveness, would find eternal mercy and rest in Him. He further instructed Faustina to become the instrument by which He would institute a new, most sanctifying Feast Day in the Church, Divine Mercy Sunday. It is through this feast that Our Lord explained to Saint Faustina, His mercy is most available to all who seek Him. "Souls who spread the honor of My mercy I shield through their entire lives as a tender mother her infant, and at the hour of death I will not be a Judge for them, but the Merciful Savior. At that last hour, a soul has nothing with which to defend itself except My mercy. Happy is the soul that during its lifetime immersed itself in the Fountain of Mercy, because justice will have no hold on it." [72] Prior to her death at the age of 33 in 1938, Jesus taught St. Faustina that His message for all the world was mercy. His unfathomable mercy was open and available to all who seek him. Learn this simple prayer, the Divine Mercy Chaplet, and pray it with faithful trust in our Lord.

How to Pray the Chaplet of Divine Mercy

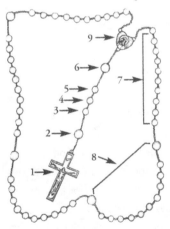

1. Make the Sign of the Cross.
2. Say the optional Opening Prayer.
3. Say the "Our Father."
4. Say the "Hail Mary."
5. Say the Apostles' Creed.
6. Say the "Eternal Father."
7. Say 10 "For the sake of His sorrowful Passion" on the "Hail Mary" beads.
8. Repeat for four more decades, saying "Eternal Father" on the "Our Father" bead and then 10 "For the sake of His sorrowful Passion" on the following "Hail Mary" beads.
9. At the conclusion of the five decades, on the medallion say the "Holy God," the concluding doxology, three times.
10. Say the optional Closing Prayer.

Used with permission of the Marian Fathers of the Immaculate Conception of the B.V.M.

[72] Saint Maria Faustina Kowalska. *Divine Mercy in My Soul*, Diary of Saint Marie Faustina Kowalska, (Marian Press, Stockbridge, MA, 2006), §1075, pg. 404.

The Divine Mercy Chaplet can also be prayed as a nine-day novena. Jesus asked Saint Faustina to focus on select souls over the nine-day novena, particularly and especially during the nine days prior to the Feast of Divine Mercy. "By this Novena I will grant every possible grace to souls". [73] Jesus asked Saint Faustina that she should bring the following souls to Him during the nine-day novena:

DAY 1: All mankind, especially sinners, and immerse them in the ocean of My mercy

DAY 2: The souls of priests and religious, and immerse them in My unfathomable mercy

DAY 3: All devout and faithful souls, and immerse them in the ocean of My mercy

DAY 4: Those who do not believe in God and those who do not yet know Me

DAY 5: The souls of those who have separated themselves from the Church

DAY 6: The meek & humble souls and the souls of little children, and immerse them in My mercy

DAY 7: The souls who especially venerate and glorify My mercy and immerse them in My mercy

DAY 8: The souls who are detained in purgatory and immerse them in the abyss of My mercy

DAY 9: Souls who have become lukewarm, and immerse them in the abyss of My mercy

Jesus further directed St. Faustina to extol the virtues of His limitless mercy, particularly at the hour of 3 pm each day. As Jesus proclaimed, "At three o'clock, implore My mercy,…immerse yourself in My Passion…This is the hour of great mercy for the whole world. I will allow you to enter into My mortal sorrow." [74] Memorialize and venerate this hour each day, the very hour of His death. If you can find a chapel at 3 pm, stop and pray. If you are unable to adore the Blessed Eucharist at this time, make time wherever you are to seek the mercy of the Lord, for a moment's time. Set your cell phone alarm for 3 pm each day, as a means to remind you of Jesus' glorious sacrifice for you and for all at this hour of the day. Take a moment, to stop and reflect on the pain He endured, the suffering He accepted, for all the world for all of time. In thanksgiving to Him and His mercy, turn to God. Make this a stop on you daily schedule and ensure your deed bead moves along.

---

[74] Saint Maria Faustina Kowalska. §1320, pg. 474.

[73] Saint Maria Faustina Kowalska. §796, pg. 316.

With deed beads in hand, take a little step throughout your day on the path to holiness. Grow in sanctity as you find a moment to reach out to your Creator in prayer. The time can be brief, it can be amidst quiet or confusion, but make a moment for your Father on a routine basis. Speak to him in prayer, as one speaks and comes to know his friends. Pray in charity for the sanctification of souls in Purgatory through recitation of St. Gertrude's humble prayer. By this means, open the gates of heaven for those confined to Purgatory and increase the body of saints who become connected with you in love and thankfulness. Pray for your enemies that the Heavenly reward might too be theirs. Pray the Rosary and more closely align yourself to the immaculate advocacy of Mary, the Mother of God. Grow connected to the Rosary that you acquire a subtle devotion to the efforts of Mary to bring peace and conversion to all the world. Read the Bible, that you come to know the Way of our Lord. Recite the Divine Mercy Chaplet that you avail yourself to the mercy of our Lord. Take a moment at 3 pm each and every day to reflect on all that Jesus has sacrificed for your salvation. Reach out to our Lord in these and other prayerful ways, each and every day. Be the effort large or small, the step by step walk towards Christ, deed bead by deed bead, will further open you to God's sanctifying grace while on your heavenly journey.

Contemplate:

1. Can I commit to set aside time during each day to settle my heart and speak to the Lord in prayer?

2. When might be a convenient time that I can spend time with the Lord on a daily basis?

3. What are some of the ways by which I can communicate and connect with Christ in prayer?

4. For whom shall I pray?

Ask Jesus to grant you a Love
like a purifying furnace, where your
poor flesh - like your poor heart - may
be consumed and cleansed of all
earthly miseries. Pray that it may
be emptied of self and filled with Him.
Ask Him to grant you a deep-seated
aversion to all that is worldly
so that you may be sustained
only by Love.[75]

BEAD TWO

Turn Away from Temptation

Slight deviations from the path set forth in the Word of God and in the Way of Christ are the inclinations of fallen man from the stain of Original Sin. The weakness of Mankind and our tendency towards sin was initiated and empowered by the actions of Adam and Eve. Sin entered the world at the behest of the head of the serpent, Satan, yet all is not forsaken. Although God facilitates our free will and stands not in the way of our choices, he willingly and persistently offers guidance in a variety of forms for us to choose right over wrong, good over evil, love over hate. God has left us His written guidance in the Holy Word. God has blessed us with the example of human holiness in the cenacle of Saints. God provides constant prodding at the helm of angels, guarding and guiding us along the way. God blesses us with the heavenly beauty of the Mother of God, who intercedes on our behalf and is a perpetual advocate for us before the Heavenly Throne. The ultimate assistance was recognized in the Word becoming Flesh. God placed himself in the footprint of Man by humanizing His Divinity. He humbled His power at the hands of Man, reconciling the weaknesses of mankind by offering His life as the ultimate sacrifice for our salvation. God has kept the gates of heaven open for us. We must thus remain persistent in our perseverance to walk the Way of our Lord. Choosing the narrow path takes constancy and commitment to the Way, the Truth, and the Life God has given us.

Though sin and death entered the world through the actions of man in the Garden of Eden, all is not lost. As Jesus taught, "In the world you will have trouble, but take courage, I have conquered the world." [76] Jesus' life was a proclamation of truth, truth to the Word of God. Jesus gave His life in order that we may have life…everlasting. For this, we must also give of ourselves for the glory of God and for the right to hear God call our name into the kingdom of Heaven. For us, it all begins with baptism. As we read in the Catechism, "Baptism not only purifies from all sins, but also makes the neophyte 'a new creature', an adopted

---

[75] St. JoseMaria Escriva. *The Way, Furrow, the Forge,* (Scepter Publishing, New York, New York) 1988, the Furrow verse 814, pg. 495.

[76] John 16:33

son of God, who has become a 'partaker of the divine nature', member of Christ and co-heir with him, and a temple of the Holy Spirit." [77] The grace of *justification* that we receive in baptism, is a sanctifying grace enabling us to fully love God, to live and act under the prompting of the Holy Spirit, and to grow in goodness. In this sacrament, we begin anew, by the grace of God, on the right path, with the right moral compass, cleansed of the inequity of the sin of fallen man. As children of God, we must utilize this Grace to overcome the temptation and sin we will encounter during our lives.

Because of our inherent weakness, we must find ways to overcome temptation. Temptation is a constant. It comes in a variety of forms and impacts every individual differently. Concupiscence is the hurdle we must strive to overcome. Concupiscence is "the human appetites or desires which remain disordered due to the temporal consequences of original sin, which remain even after Baptism, and which produce an inclination to sin." [78] St. Paul recognized the hidden scourge of concupiscence when he proclaimed the ongoing battle of the "flesh" against the "spirit." "For the flesh has desires against the Spirit, and the Spirit against the flesh; these are opposed to each other so that you may not do what you want." [79] St. Paul goes on to instruct the Galatians, as well as us today, that the wants of the flesh, such as: immorality, impurity, hatred, jealousy, selfishness, and envy, to name a few, are juxtaposed to Christ's message of love, joy, peace, patience, kindness, faithfulness, self-control. [80] The battle is on and we must seek to overcome, to walk the Way of Christ.

In our struggle to overcome the frailty and weaknesses of human nature, we must turn to Christ for strength. We must recognize temptations in our lives and find a means to overcome them, for the glory of God and for the salvation of our souls. Just as St. Paul proselytized about the need to persevere in faith, so too did Christ lament the weaknesses of Man while with His apostles in the Garden of Gethsemane, as His arrest was advancing, "the spirit is willing, but the flesh is weak." [81] Let us not fall asleep on Christ, but remain vigilant in our intentions and practice to

---

[77] *CCC* 1265

[78] *CCC* pg. 871.

[79] Galatians 5:17

[80] Galatians 5:19-22

[81] Matthew 26:41

overcome sin and temptation in our daily lives. Step by step, little way by little way. Overcoming temptation begins with the heart. The heart will guide your moral compass as the "seat of moral personality." [82] As Jesus instructed in the Sermon on the Mount in the sixth of the Beatitudes, "Blessed are the clean of heart, for they shall see God." [83] Seeing God in the beatific vision is only accomplished when centered with a heart of purity. We must strive to be centered in holiness with a respect toward charity, chastity, love of truth and orthodoxy of faith. These are the demands of our Heavenly Father for an eternal relationship in love. Begin with the end in mind, with an understanding of the precondition for a life of love with our Father, a pure heart.

The process of purifying the heart can be accomplished, by the grace of God, through the practice of "little ways." Making an effort to turn away from temptations, and thus avoiding sin, can be a gradual practice in learned behavior, a behavior that practices the Way of our Lord. Identify simple temptations during your day, things that draw you into the belly of the serpent, causing us to turn our backs on our Father. Using your deed beads, find opportunities to avoid sin and temptation, and to offer goodness and purity of heart to our Father. Slide a bead when you are successful in turning the tide and offering goodness and love to God. Little by little, grow in purity and come to turn your back on Satan and sin.

Today's temptations often run afoul of the 9th and 10th Commandments. A covetness of another's person, as lust, or another's goods, as envy, are steps on the path to Satan's door. Offenses against numbers 9 and 10 in the Commands of our Father represent a direct affront to the purity of one's heart. For example, seeing an attractive stranger and opening the door for lust is a common crack in the armor of chastity. Seeing just such a beautiful soul is an opportunity to offer love to God. Turn away from such a soul and do not see them by the limits of their physical beauty. Turn aside and avoid the temptation and offer this gift to God…slide a bead. Alternatively, see them for their beauty and uniqueness and be thankful to God for their health and well-being. As such, take a temptation for lust and turn it into an offering of love and thanks to our Lord. Similarly, in observing the blessings of your neighbor's successes or possessions, let not the sin of envy win the day. Rather, find joy in your neighbor's delight and praise God for his

---

[82] *CCC* 2517
[83] Matthew 5:8

goodness and your neighbor's satisfaction. Let the bead move from here to there as you practice purity of heart in your tempting encounters of lust or envy. Let the beauty or the success of another become an opportunity to not only avoid sin, but to take delight in their good fortune. Offer this goodness in thanksgiving to God and grow in purity.

Chastity is routinely attacked by the barrage of impurity in today's society. Television commercials and shows, magazine covers and articles, pornography at the stroke of a computer key, all represent the seductions of Satan, calling for destruction from atop the highest mountain, yet in the lowliest of places. Our world today is a burlesque show of the highest order, yet in the subtlest of ways. Let not your heart be corrupted. Turn the channel, forego the article, choose wisely on the worldwide web, that your purity remains intact. Choose chastity over corruption. Practice little ways to holiness. Draw a bead closer on your deed bead strand as you choose purity of heart over the negative impact of today's impurity.

Similarly, when it comes to our attire, practice the purity that Christ preaches. Modesty in dress is becoming a lost treasure in the troves of today's wardrobes. Over exposure of God's gifts of one's physicality is a beacon for impurity. It is commonplace for men and women to succumb to the temptations of beauty and to travel the corridors of Satan's lair. Modesty is a virtue by which one acknowledges the sexual weaknesses of another. Dress in a manner that does not exploit such weaknesses as such immodesty can become an unnecessary source of temptation. [84] As Christ proclaimed, "Everyone who looks at a woman with lust has already committed adultery with her in his heart." [85] Women, however, are no less guilty of the fleeting pleasures of sin by their tempting solicitations. For women, choose modesty as a means to purity. Grow in purity and charity not only for yourself, but also for the male souls you encounter. "Modesty protects the intimate center of the person. It means refusing to unveil what should remain hidden." [86] By one's choice in clothing, particularly rooted in temperance and modesty, one can practice a resistance to the allure of today's fashion and encourage purity for both man and woman in the art of relationships. Practice *Little Ways to Little Sanctity* by choosing modesty in one's appearance.

---

[84] John and Sheila Kippley, *Natural Family Planning, The Complete Approach.* pg 20.

[85] Matthew 5:28

[86] *CCC* 2521

Sinful emotions are found not only in lust, but in anger as well. Understand that sin reproduces sin and reinforces itself. Sin begets a proclivity towards sin. [87] In order to overcome the sin of anger, so prevalent in our self-centered society, we must safeguard ourselves in peace. For we acknowledge and believe Christ's words that "blessed are the peacemakers, for they shall be called sons of God". [88] A demeanor ordered in peace further begets a self centered in peace and parcels out this gift to all one's acquaintances. Jesus gave the gift of peace to all those he encountered, whether friend or foe. By His blood on the Cross, for all mankind, Christ overcame persecution, hostility and sin for the benefit of all. He became the Prince of Peace. [89] We too must seek peace in our day.

Assess your actions in this regard. Anger can be subtle and anger can be pronounced. Seek control of your emotions towards God's princely souls. Each is unique and in His image. Each life is sacred to God. [90] Seek *Little Ways to Little Sanctity* by finding peace in times where Satan offers anger. Today's roadways and shopping malls are fraught with anger. Being cut off by a passing driver can entice an evil thought or scowl. The ravages of consumerism can lead to unhealthy thoughts of fellow shoppers or shop-keepers. This is subtle anger of which we are all profoundly guilty. Through your little ways, become a prince of peace. During such episodes where anger and hostility can arise, make a commitment to peace and a change of heart. On the roadways when encountering another aggressive driver, look away and do not succumb to enraged emotions. Offer a brief prayer of goodwill for the sake of that driver. Find peace in your heart. When overcome by frustration in the malls of America, seek comfort in docility amongst your fellow shoppers. Let not your feelings turn to anger in times of rush or frustration, but present them to our Lord as an offering of peace and goodwill. Each expression of peace, in overcoming anger, merits a deed amongst your beads. Allow these little offerings, these little ways, to bring you to God, to bring you closer to holiness.

The sin of gossip similarly opens us to a life of discord and can become destructive to the lives of others as well. In gossip, we come to exalt our very being over the

---

[87] *CCC* 1865

[88] Matthew 5:9

[89] Isaiah 9:5

[90] *CCC* 2258

uniqueness of another. We bring judgment to the foreground when we are asked to leave it to God. God's Eighth Command is to not bear false witness against our neighbor. With this comes the obligation and responsibility to be truthful in our discourse and leave judgment and gossip behind. God has manifested His truth in His Son, Jesus Christ. Jesus Christ came to bear witness to the truth, to all mankind. Jesus' life is a testament to the truth of His Heavenly Father. Jesus testified to Pilate and to all, that He is Truth and he brings it to all.[91] Our Catechism teaches the need to ensure respect for reputation. One becomes guilty of "rash judgment" when one assumes as true, without sufficient foundation, the moral fault of another. One becomes guilty of "detraction" when one discloses the faults and failings of another to persons for whom these are unknown. One becomes guilty of "calumny" when one harms the reputation of another and gives occasion to false judgment.[87] So, guard your tongue. Let not the temptations of Satan lead you to judgment and gossip of others. When occasions for gossip or judgment arise, become childlike and humble in your thoughts. Bear witness to the truth, as Christ is the truth. Turn away from occasions of gossip and judgment and relish the little step along the narrow path towards holiness.

We must also be aware of our attractions not only to others, to other's goods, or consideration of other's reputation, but we must also gain hold of our own interior emotions with respect to the goods of the world. We must seek not to become ensconced in a need for possessions. Be leery of an unusual attraction to the goods of the world for this insatiation can become unremitting. More begets more, big begets bigger, and better begets best. The thirst for worldly attractions can become insatiable. Understand that the fruits of God's earth are for the common stewardship of all mankind. It is legitimate to seek to obtain the comforts of property to the extent of meeting our basic needs. Hold firm however, for respect for human dignity "requires the practice of the virtue of temperance, so as to moderate attachment to this world's goods."[93] We must recognize that God is the gifter of all our worldly goods and we are called, with God's grace, to mortify our earthly cravings and "prevail over the seductions of pleasure and power."[94] In our advanced society and in the context of advanced consumerism, we encounter new and better at every turn. We are exposed to

---

[91] John 18:37

[92] CCC 2477

[93] CCC 2407

the latest model of cars. We find the newest style of clothes among the grandest of stores. We can shop for food in the most exclusive of markets. We must ask ourselves however, what and how much is beyond our need? Can we practice temperance in the arena of temptation? Can we find a "little way" to avoid our over indulgence? We can, step by step, little way by little way. As the Catholic *Catechism* guides, "All Christ's faithful are to direct their affections rightly, lest they be hindered in their pursuit of perfect charity by the use of worldly things and by an adherence to riches which is contrary to the spirit of evangelical poverty." [95]

Thus, the little way of St. Thérèse, a practice in humility and temperance, can advance our pursuit of littleness and our growth in holiness. Recognize Satan's snares in your daily routine and seek to anticipate your areas of weakness and navigate your emotions in God's direction. Turn away from temptations of the eyes and avoid envious emotions towards your neighbor. Moderate your dress so as not to corrupt the chastity and purity of others. Turn anger into purity and judge not your neighbor's faults. Seek what you need, but use not what is in excess. Walk in the Way of Christ and grow in purity of heart. Give to God the fullness of your being and turn Satan's traps into opportunities to advance your love for Christ and for your neighbor.

[94] *CCC* 2549
[95] *CCC* 2545, pg. 609 as *Lumen Gentium* 42 §3.

Contemplate:

1. Are there specific temptations with which I struggle or to which I find myself succumbing more often than others?

2. What might be some actions that I can proactively take to avoid those reoccurring temptations?

3. What are some of the things I can do to avoid giving in to those temptations when I am being challenged?

4. What are some of the ways that I can allow Jesus to support me and help me to avoid temptation?

When you have finished your work,
do your brother's, helping him, for the
sake of Christ, with such finesse
and naturalness that no one—
not even he—will realize that you are
doing more that in justice you ought.
This, indeed, is virtue befitting a
son of God! [96]

BEAD THREE

Be Charitable

Giving gifts to our Lord on the road to holiness can also involve the physical gifting of ourselves to our neighbor. With the grace of God's gift of love, we are called to charity which "perfects all means of sanctification." [92] As Christ taught a life of love, He enjoined His apostles, with the fulfillment of the Holy Spirit, on a life lived in sanctity. The Disciple's help spread His Church, the Church of Christ, which He founded upon a community of life lived in love and a community of life in holiness. The Body of Christ, His Church, nurtured saints and martyrs who struggled with sin yet, by the grace of God, were conquerors. As Blessed Pope Paul VI described in the Solemn Profession of Faith, "the Church is therefore holy, though having sinners in her midst, because she herself has no other life but the life of grace. If they live her life, her members are sanctified; if they move away from her life, they fall into sins and disorders that prevent the radiation of her sanctity." [98] It is just such a life of love, for the community of others, that becomes manifest in the beautiful gift of charity.

Our profession of faith is our response to God's invitation to holiness. In seeking God, perseverance and a heightening of our faith is achieved through our response to God's invitation, in charity. Charity is our active demonstration of the faith we hold in our heart and God's call for each of us to "love one another as I love you." [99] Charity is an act not of servitude, but of love. This gift of Christ that he passed on to His disciples through the strength of the Holy Spirit, and for which His Church and its members built a foundation upon, is rooted in His teaching "Let charity be genuine...Love one another with brotherly affection". [100] Christ projected the full force of His love and affection for the lost sheep. As Christ revealed in the story of the prodigal son, His love was always manifest and alive in the relationship

---

[96] St. JoseMaria Escriva. *The Way, Furrow, the Forge,* (Scepter Publishing, New York, New York) 1988, the Way verse 440, pg. 107.

[97] *CCC* 826, pg. 218 as *Lumen Gentium* 42.

[98] *CCC* 827, pg. 219 as *Solemn Profession of Faith:* Credo of the People of God §19.

[99] John 15:12

[100] *Catechism* §1971, pg. 479 as Lumen Gentium 42.

between the Father and his loving son. However, it was to the Father's lost child, his prodigal son, that he ran out to meet and embrace on his coming home. In the Father's embrace was all that he had. It was His love, it was his finest robes and richest rings, it was His fattest calf. So too must we extend all that we have in charity for the coming home of our friend, our neighbor, and even our enemy. "If your enemy is hungry, feed him; if he is thirsty, give him something to drink... Do not be conquered by evil but conquer evil with good." [101] Give a heart of purity, with a charitable gifting to those in need.

Charity is our public call to holiness. Christ taught us to give of our very selves, in the fullness of faith, to our brothers and sisters in need. The disadvantaged, whether friend or foe, need us to be instruments of our Lord and respond to their call for comfort. "Amen, I say to you, whatever you did to one of these least brothers of mine, you did for me." [102] As revealed to St. Catherine of Siena, God purposely did not distribute gifts and virtues equally amongst all men. Some shall principally have humility, others justice, another faith, and still others may be in want. However, God calls all to His holiness through charity to others that we might all be fulfilled. [103] In charity, we are called to render to God that which He asks and expects us to give to our neighbor. For all Christ's faithful are to "direct their affections rightly, lest they be hindered in their pursuit of perfect charity by the use of worldly things and by an adherence to riches which is contrary to the spirit of evangelical poverty." [104]

On the narrow road before us, seek a path in holiness founded on charity. In a life inspired in self-giving, for the good of others, we become a counter ballast to the prevalence of selfishness and pride so pronounced in our world. We become an instrument of God's gift of grace for the good of all. Let your heart grow in purity, for from a pure heart does charity reign. [105] As Jesus instructed Sister Faustina in her learnings on the unfathomable mercy He has to offer for all, Jesus proclaimed His want for all to exercise mercy for others. Jesus' first instruction in this regard

---

[101] Romans 12:20-21

[102] Matthew 25:40

[103] *CCC* 1937, pg. 470 as St. Catherine of Siena, *Dial.* I, 7.

[104] *Lumen Gentium* 42, §3.

[105] *CCC* 1794, pg. 441.

[106] Saint Maria Faustina Kowalska. §742, pg. 297.

was to express mercy to one's neighbor in deed.[106] Do for them, give to them, seek to bring comfort to others. In so doing, not only are you becoming holy in your actions, you are abiding by Jesus' call for us to be "poor in spirit", humble, and charitable in our gifts. Jesus asks for us to be charitable and live a life of self-giving, "Whoever seeks to preserve his life will lose it, but whoever loses it will save it." [107]

Almsgiving is a clear manifestation of the call to charity that Christ asks of all on the narrow road to holiness. In the Corporal Works of Mercy, we all are called to action as children of God, living in communion with our brethren. We are called to feed the hungry, shelter the homeless, clothe the naked, visit the sick and imprisoned and bury the dead. Jesus asks us to give to those in need, "Whoever has two cloaks should share with the person who has none. And whoever has food should do likewise". [108] Many in the cenacle of saints walked this road, a life lived in giving and in sacrifice for the lowly and the down-trodden. St. Rose of Lima explained her charitable actions for the poor, "when we serve the poor and the sick, we serve Jesus. We must not fail to help our neighbors, because in them we serve Jesus." [109]

In your reach towards sanctity, little step by little step, find ways to give to those in need. In the passing of the basket at Mass, for special collections, give not only your heart in prayer, but also of your money to bring comfort to those in need. Our Catholic brethren in the missions live the call to charity on the front lines of poverty and need our financial support and resources to extend the helping hand of Christ's Church. To them, be charitable. Sponsoring a child through a charitable organization is another way to use your financial resources to feed the hungry. A token gift can be so meaningful for the impoverished. Setting out a collection jar at home can become a subtle reminder of the constant need and can become a means to donate money from amongst your spare change. Almsgiving is an avenue that is always open to us in our walk with Christ. In the pains of the poor, Jesus highlighted the gift of true love for those in need when he described the poor widow's alms from amongst her need. "Amen I say to you, this poor widow put in more than all the other contributors to the treasury. For they have all

---

[107] Luke 17:33

[108] Luke 3:11

[109] CCC 2449, pg. 589 as P. Hansen, Vita mirabilis (Louvain, 1668).

contributed from their surplus wealth, but she, from her poverty, has contributed all she had, her whole livelihood." [110]

Your almsgiving can involve more than just the gifting of money, find goods amongst your possessions that would serve those in need. The impoverished, the unemployed, the despondent, can find joy and peace through the receipt of goods whose meaning to us has become lost amongst our worldly possessions. Clothes, winter coats or boots, and toys are examples of items at your fingertips that can bring unbelievable joy to a single parent seeking to enrich the lives of their child. Let your excess be a miracle to the want of those in need. Be the good Samaritan that Christ calls us to be. Be the instrument of peace that Christ wants to fulfill through our blessings. Become present in spirit for the good of others by the selfless giving of your goods to one in need.

Give in charity of your time to the body of Christ, to the community of mankind. Volunteering of one's time in visiting the infirmed, teaching the less educated, counseling the anxious, or serving those in need becomes an active expression of your faith in Christ and your love for your neighbor. Your fraternal charity is a proclamation of the depths of your love for Him that came to attend to the lost sheep. You become a Samaritan to the injured, a father to the lost son, a shepherd to the lamb. Your sacrifice is an expression of your inherent sanctity for with "holy actions, the laity consecrate the world itself to God, everywhere offering worship by the holiness of their lives." [111] You become holy by the sacrifice you make for the good of another. "Every action done so as to cling to God in communion of holiness, and thus achieved blessedness, is a true sacrifice." [112]

In our lives, charity becomes the will of God put into action. Open your eyes, and your heart, to the needs of your friend, to the needs of your foe. Give to he that is in want as did the Lamb of God give of Himself to the needs of all mankind. "Do not be conquered by evil, conquer evil with good." [108] Let Christ in the Eucharist strengthen your charity. Let the call of the needy be heard in your reply. Let the holiness that resides in the purity of your heart lead a call to action. "If we obey

---

[110] Mark 12:43-44

[111] CCC 901, pg. 238 as Lumen Gentium 34.

[112] CCC 2099, pg. 509 as St. Augustine, De civ. Dei 10, 6.

[113] Romans 12:21

for the sake of the good itself and out of love for him who commands…we are in the position of children." [114] Become child-like in your charitable humility and draw a bead as you give to your neighbor in need.

Giving is the heart of charity. As Christ taught, "Amen, I say to you, whatever you did for one of these least brothers of mine, you did for me." [115] Mercy is another way we can give of ourselves and our heart to our neighbor. Mercy is a restoration of communion with God and community with neighbor. Pope Francis declared the pastoral year beginning in 2015 as the Jubilee of Mercy. Pope Francis has professed "the commitment to live by mercy so as to obtain the grace of complete and exhaustive forgiveness by the power of the love of the Father who excludes no one. The Jubilee Indulgence is thus full, the fruit of the very event which is to be celebrated and experienced with faith, hope and charity." [116] Mercy is a gift shared with us by our merciful Father and for which we, in the charity of our love, can share with others. We are called to show that mercy can overcome anger. We are called to loosen the rigidity of our heart towards our neighbor. Let the spark of Christ's Divinity bring light where there has been darkness. Let us focus on the logo of the Jubilee of Mercy that we may practice what it presents.

[www.iubilaeummisericordiae.va]

---

[114] *CCC* 1828, pg. 450 as St. Basil, *Reg. fus. tract.,* prol.3: J.P. Migne, ed., Patrologia Graeca (Paris, 1857-1866).

[115] Matthew 25:40

[116] Pope Francis, September 2015, www.im.va.

"The motto Merciful Like the Father (taken from the Gospel of Luke, 6:36) serves as an invitation to follow the merciful example of the Father who asks us not to judge or condemn but to forgive and to give love and forgiveness without measure." [117]

Christ challenges us to not only practice mercy, but to profess His mercy. In charity, we should bring Christ's forgiveness to our brethren. As Christ explained to Saint Faustina, "All those souls who will glorify My mercy and spread its worship, encouraging others to trust in My mercy, will not experience terror at the hour of death. My mercy will shield them in that final battle." [118] Mercy shall be given freely and we must seek to profess Christ's mercy and to practice the cleansing of these life-giving waters. In the act of mercy, we hold an olive branch waiting to be extended to our foe in need. We can become a disciple of Christ as we practice the mercy He gave to the world.

Our deed beads can be an instrument to help us profess mercy as we practice *Little Ways to Little Sanctity*. In the quite of our hearts, we can relinquish the grip of anger and resentment, and sow a seed of love and forgiveness. Allow mercy to bring restoration to relationships that have suffered. We are all God's children and we can take a little step towards holiness with each charitable act of love and forgiveness.

---

[117] Pope Francis, May 5, 2015; www.im.va.

[118] Saint Maria Faustina Kowalska. §1540, pg. 547.

Contemplate:

1. Am I satisfied with the level of charity and mercy I display in my life?

2. How and when can I be more charitable and display greater mercy?

3. Is there someone or something that I need to make a deeper commitment to in my display of acting in charity or in mercy?

4. How can I be a role-model to others about Christ's call to charity and mercy?

*Don't aspire to be like the gilded weather
vane on top of a great building. However
much it may glitter, however high it may be,
it adds nothing to the firmness of the
structure. Rather be like an old stone block
hidden in the foundations, under the
ground where no one can see you.
Because of you, the house will not fall.* [119]

*I advise you not to look for praise, even when
you deserve it. It is better to pass unnoticed,
and to let the most beautiful and noble aspects
of our actions, of our lives, remain hidden.
What a great thing it is to become little!
Deo omnis Gloria! - All the glory to God.* [120]

BEAD FOUR

Humble Yourself, Become Little

The Catholic Catechism brings to life all that Christ asks of us in its definition of *Humility:* "the virtue by which a Christian acknowledges that God is the author of all good. Humility avoids inordinate ambition or pride, and provides the foundation for turning to God in prayer. Voluntary humility can be described as 'poverty of spirit.'" [121] As the life in our being, the silence amongst the noise, the breeze that makes all things move, our Father is it. I AM is more than we can comprehend and more than we can put into words. He is the essence of all that we are as we are of His likeness, [122] but so very much more. Recognizing the Creator amongst His creation is our call in life, to seek Him in all that we do, to give to Him the love that we have to offer. All glory is His.

In the third chapter of the Bible, in Genesis where all life began at the hand of the Divine, we first encounter the destruction that can ensue in our lives when we fail to recognize the Glory of God in the Highest. Satan alienated himself from the love of God by his refusal to exercise a humble heart with a love for the Father as He should be loved. Lucifer's fall from grace and banishment from the Kingdom is manifest in his wish for the destruction of all Man out of a pride of self, maintaining an erroneous and sinful belief in an equality with our God. The serpent introduces this destruction by tempting the Woman, Eve, with the Original error, "the serpent said to the woman: 'You certainly will not die!' No, God knows well that the moment you eat of it your eyes will be opened and you will be like gods who know what is good and what is bad." [123] The one truth herein lies in the testament that in the fall of Man, their eyes were indeed opened. They were opened to the sin of pride and the want of humility "then the eyes of both of them were opened, and they realized that they were naked." [124]

---

[119] St. JoseMaria Escriva. *The Way, Furrow, the Forge,* (Scepter Publishing, New York, New York) 1988, the Way verse 590, pg. 147.

[120] St. JoseMaria Escriva. *The Way, Furrow, the Forge,* (Scepter Publishing, New York, New York) 1988, the Forge verse 1051, pg. 842.

[121] *CCC* pg. 882.

[122] Genesis 1:27

[123] Genesis 3:4-5

[124] Genesis 3:7

Thankfully, God has blessed the world with giants amongst the community of the faithful. In their faithfulness and humility to the greatness of our God, the foundation of our faith gained root. The seeds were being sown throughout the course of history, to prepare the world for the truth that Christ would reveal. Stewards of God's greatness, opened their minds and their hearts to the love of the Father and the graces he sought to bestow. Humble servants came before the Lord and accepted the path that the Father had prepared for them to lead Man back to the heart of the Divine through humility.

Abraham walked in faith at the voice of the Lord. He "walk(ed) by faith, not by sight". [125] Abraham loved the Lord so fully and completely, that he willingly prepared the sacrifice of his son at God's command. Out of this humble act, Abraham secured the favor of the Most High, "because you acted as you did in not withholding from me your beloved son, I will bless you abundantly and make your descendants as countless as the stars of the sky and the sands of the seashore...all this because you obeyed my command." [126] We all are here today, as descendants of Abraham, our patriarch, who led the world in humility and out of love for his Creator. He is our Father in faith.

So too did faith result in the greatness of Moses' humble actions before the throne of the mighty Pharaoh of Egypt. Moses recognized the weakness of his own character, but in faithfulness, he answered the call of the Heavenly Father. "I am a poor speaker, how can it be that Pharaoh will listen to me?" [127] Through the hand of the almighty, Moses captured the attention of the King of Egypt, eventually bringing him to his knees before the power of God. Moses took the needs of all of the Israelites upon his shoulders and carried their burdens to safety. After questioning his abilities to achieve the will of the Father, "only after long debate does Moses attune his will to that of the Savior God," [128] does Moses come to understand his littleness, and in faith he becomes the mouthpiece of the Lord.

John the Baptist is first stirred to movement before the presence of the Blessed

---

[125] 2 Corinthians 5:7

[126] Genesis 22:16-18

[127] Exodus 6:30

[128] CCC 2575

[129] Luke 1:41

Virgin as the "infant leaped in her womb" [129] upon the magnificent encounter of Mary and Elizabeth. In joy, John celebrates the presence of the Lord who is carried in the womb of the New Ark of the Covenant. As a prophet and merely "the voice of one crying out in the desert", [130] John understands and proclaims his littleness before the faithful, "I baptize with water, but there is one among you whom you do not recognize, the one who is coming after me, whose sandal strap I am not worthy to untie." [131] As the last of the prophets of the Old Covenant, John is driven to prepare the way for He that is to come. His joy has been made complete and John instructs his followers "he must increase; I must decrease." [132]

The Blessed Virgin, the apex of human humility, sacrifices all for the glory of God. She risks abandonment from Joseph and she risks death at the hands of her townspeople. Despite fear and confusion from this lowly child of God, Mary offers all that she has. "Behold, I am the handmaid of the Lord. May it be done to me according to your word." [133] She willingly becomes the instrument of the Most High, the vessel through which the world will be saved. She comes to understand that she is destined for a life of pain and sacrifice, "and you yourself a sword will pierce", [134] yet she turns not from the turmoil ahead, but accompanies her Son, the Messiah of Mankind, through His travels in Galilee, through the streets of Jerusalem, to the hill of His glorious triumph. She remains fully attuned to the plight of Man and the salvation that Her Son came to offer, even as she suffers with Him at the foot of His cross.

The humility of Joseph is found not in the brevity of his actions as given to us through the Word of God, but in his simple, yet magnanimous gift to the world in ushering in the infant Jesus for all the world to behold. Faced with the knowledge of Mary's condition, "he did as the angel of the Lord had commanded him and took his wife into his home." [135] He led Mary, with Child, to the seat of prophesy for God's entrance to unfold "and you, Bethlehem, land of Judah, are by no means least among the rulers of Judah; since from you shall come a ruler, who is to

---

[130] John 1:23

[131] John 1:26-27

[132] John 3:30

[133] Luke 1:38

[134] Luke 2:35

[135] Matthew 1:24

shepherd my people Israel." [136]   At God's command, Joseph brought comfort to his spouse and protection for the Infant King. He led the Holy Family to safety through the sands of Egypt and at the announced time, he followed the precedent of obedience and humility that Moses revealed many centuries before in the exodus from Egypt, as he brought forth the Messiah that the prophecy might further be fulfilled "Out of Egypt I called my son." [137] In a lasting moment of love, Joseph brings forth the Son for His presentation before His Father in the Temple in Jerusalem. The patriarch Joseph led the Blessed Virgin and Infant King in a spirit of simpleness and obedience that their holy mission might be fulfilled.

From the Middle Ages emerged one of the most humble and loved of all God's saints, Saint Francis of Assisi. Saint Francis was a rebellious youth who came from a family of wealth. However, in his early twenties, Francis was moved by the call of the Father to relinquish his comforts and follow in the way of the Lord. Francis gave all his wealth away to the beggars and the impoverished, and solemnly joined their ranks. Stories abound about the pure and humble man that Francis came to be as he sought simpleness and unity to the word and spirit of Christ's love. Francis later organized his new order of Franciscans, friars who were committed to follow the teachings of Jesus Christ and to walk in His footsteps. In 1224, Francis received the mark of the stigmata and became the first recorded person to physically bear the miraculous markings of the wounds of Christ. His humility was renowned and was exemplified by the story of him switching clothes with a local beggar and taking up his place amongst the street urchins. Often attributed to St. Francis, he indeed left us much in the way of lessons in humility in the great yet simple prayer that introduces us to his simple love for our Lord: "Lord, make me an instrument of your peace, where there is hatred, let me sow love..." [138]

A lesser known saint among the symphony of God's earthly mortal treasures is the simple servant Saint Germaine Cousins. [139]   Born and raised in France in the late 1500's, Germaine bore the mark of imperfection by her withered hand and her feeble physique. Germaine was ostracized by her stepmother and relegated to a life lived in the cold and dampness of the family barn. Never to set foot in the

---

[137] Matthew 2:15

[138] Prayer of St. Francis

[139] http://www.catholicnewsagency.com/saint.php?n=497

[136] Matthew 2:6

house of her family and shunned by her father, the loving embrace of her heavenly family did not tend to her until after her death at 22 years of age. This simple yet beautiful virgin soul found solace and contentment in her meek and humble living quarters and peacefully and thankfully accepted her meals outside on the doorstep of her family's home. Her Cinderella-like life was harsh and demanding, yet she never missed her daily morning mass and her only book on life was found in the rosary. Germaine's humility and sincerity captured the attention of all the surrounding children, who gathered daily while she tended her sheep to hear her words of love and her instructions on the calling of the Father. When publicly indicted by her stepmother at the town-square for hoarding and stealing food in her apron, the miraculous appearance and display of flowers amongst her apron pockets testified to the love she always bore amongst her surrounding afflictions. St. Germaine Cousins was a testament to humility and to love, especially for those who had abandoned her in affection.

From the doorstep of St. Germaine Cousins to the doorstep of Canada's College of Notre Dame, humility could further be found. Saint Andre Bessette was an uneducated disciple with great love for the Master and a great devotion to His foster father, St. Joseph.[140] Andre Bessette was assigned to the task of doorkeeper at the College, and he humbly served in this uninviting capacity for over forty years. A brother of the Congregation of the Holy Cross, Brother Andre was known for his great love for all who came to his door. He found food for the hungry and provided comfort to those in need. His life away from his door was filled with service through the simple tasks of washing floors and windows, cleaning lamps, and bringing in firewood. Though simple in intellect, he was grand in love and humility, particularly for those in need. He sought the least as he was the least. He loved the lowly as he was the lowly. He checked his pride and his ambition, and truly became the essence of what Christ described in the blessings of those with poverty of spirit, for the kingdom of heaven shall be theirs. [141]

A perfect humility in littleness and love for Jesus can be found on into modern times. The Little Flower, Saint Thérèse, who introduced us to her Little Ways, sought Jesus in all that she did. An ordinary girl, Thérèse came to show extraordinary love for Christ throughout her day and throughout her life. Whether it be by fast

---

[140] http://www.ewtn.com/library/MARY/BROANDRE.htm
[141] Matthew 5:3

or by sacrifice, Thérèse grew in sanctity before the eyes of her cloistered sisters. She wrote, "Jesus does not demand great actions from us but simply surrender and gratitude." [142] She lived a love spoken of in Wisdom for those who are little mercy shall be shown [143] and in Proverbs let the little ones come to the Father. [144] Thérèse sought to enlighten souls and welcomed martyrdom if it but brought mercy and salvation to her brethren. She willingly became a sacrifice for others and came to fulfill the words of St. John of the Cross on behalf of Mother Church, "the smallest act of pure love is of more value to her than all other works together." [145] Her extreme love for Christ was poured out to satisfy His thirst. Even today, her gift remains through her advocacy for souls from on high.

Maria Faustina Kowalska, Saint Faustina, enjoined her life to the passion and suffering of our Lord. This twentieth century saint became a giant in our faith through her sacrifice and through her littleness. She prayed, "I want to become a sacrificial host before You, but an ordinary wafer to people. I want the fragrance of my sacrifice to be known to You alone." [146] She relished the idea of advancing in St. Ignatius' third degree of humility, to not only refrain from defending oneself when reproached or ridiculed, but to rejoice in this humiliation. [147] She preferred to be a "lowly drudge in the convent than a queen in the world." [148] Saint Faustina brought to the world the Feast of Divine Mercy, revealed to her by the merciful Messiah, and she came to personify the littleness He sought in all souls. Her life filled with a true and pure love of Jesus is captured in her Diary during the Easter Season of 1936: "O, what joy it is to empty myself for the sake of immortal souls! I know that the grain of wheat must be destroyed and ground between millstones in order to become food. In the same way, I must become destroyed in order to be useful to the Church and souls, even though exteriorly no one will notice my sacrifice. O Jesus, outwardly, I want to remain hidden, just like this little wafer wherein the eye perceives nothing, and yet I am a host consecrated to You." [149]

The world marveled at the littleness, simplicity and humility that Mother Teresa showed in love to all the least of God's children. Now called by the name

---

[142] Steven Payne. *The Carmelite Tradition: Spirituality in History* (2011), pg 119.

[143] Wisdom 6:7

[144] Proverbs 9:4

[145] Spiritual Canticle, stanza 29, no. 2, Collected Works, pg. 587; St. Thérèse of Lisieux. *The Story of a Soul: The Autobiography of Saint Thérèse of Lisieux*, pg. 197.

[146] Sister Sophia Michalenko. *The Life of Faustina Kowalska*, (Franciscan Media) pg. 110.

Saint Teresa of Calcutta, she left the safety and comfort of the Sisters of Loreto convent to walk a path that has become the Missionaries of Charity. Called by God to live amongst the poor and the forgotten, Saint Mother Teresa became a living instrument of God's peace and His love for the lowly. Saint Teresa of Calcutta captured the world's attention by her unwavering and tireless crusade to bring comfort to those in pain, nourishment to those in want. Saint Teresa of Calcutta joined the ranks of the impoverished to align her sacrifice with theirs in a life lived amongst the poor and to live a life of service to God's children. Saint Teresa of Calcutta taught the world the good that was found in the impoverished, the peace that each person could offer to those in need, and the love that God asks of us to share to the least of His brethren. Her life in humble service to the Lord was guided by His hand and dedicated to bringing His love to "the hungry, the naked, the homeless, the crippled, the blind, the lepers, all those people who feel unwanted, unloved, uncared for throughout society, people that have become a burden to the society and are shunned by everyone." [150]

These are just a few examples of the symphony of souls that the Almighty conductor has orchestrated throughout time, demonstrating for all the world to see that a simple, humble son or daughter of God, open to His graces, can create a melody of love. The sanctity they have attained is not a sanctity in greatness, but rather in littleness. These are but a few of the jewels found amongst the corridors of time that have heard and accepted the call of the Father. Their ways, and that of all the saints, is also the way of our Lord, a life lived in humble obedience to the Father. A life lived in the world, but not of the world.

Jesus spoke very poignantly of the call to be a humble servant. He instructed His disciples that upon His departure, they would need to walk in His footsteps. As the leaders of His Church, they were being called to wash the feet of all mankind through love, through patience, through compassion, through humility. "Amen, amen, I say to you, no slave is greater than his master nor any messenger greater than the one who sent him." [151] The Master came that we might know the ways

---

[147] Sister Sophia Michalenko, pg. 72.

[148] Saint Maria Faustina Kowalska. §254, pg. 125.

[149] Saint Maria Faustina Kowalska. §641, pg. 266.

[150] Paul Williams. (2002). *Mother Teresa.* (Indianapolis. Alpha Books, 2002) pg. 62.

[151] John 13:16

of His Father. In humility, he was rejected by His townspeople for the sake of truth. In humility, He washed the feet of His disciples that we might know love. In humility, He accepted death on a cross for Man that we might know mercy.

Imagine a beautiful spring day, resting on the side of a hill awash in the glow of the sun, with the gentle whisper of the wind and the lapping of the water along the shore. It may have been just such a day where a Teacher with a captivating countenance brought forth a lesson that as of yet had been untold. He spoke of love and He spoke of sacrifice. He spoke of simpleness and He spoke of humility. He brought a message of love that the world needed to hear and needed to understand. His ways were not our ways. His ways were God's ways! "Offer no resistance to one who is evil. When someone strikes you on your right cheek, turn the other one to him as well." [152] "Should anyone press you into service for one mile, go with him for two miles. Give to the one who asks of you, and do not turn your back on one who wants to borrow." [153] This is the love and the humility of the Lord, the love and the humility He is asking of us! He taught further and deeper, do not be judgmental of others that we too might not be judged. Do not serve two masters. Do not seek treasures that are transient and only of this world, that they will be gone in the next. Love your enemy as yourself. Give to those in need. Forgive others as the Heavenly Father will forgive you. Do not be of the world, but be in the world. Take the gifts and graces you have been given and use them fruitfully for the benefit of others. Be a shining light of love for all the world. The luminescence of each of us may be different, but send forth your essence of love for all the world to receive. Be a ray of hope, be a ray of peace! "When Jesus finished these words, the crowds were astonished at his teaching, for he taught them as one having authority, and not as their scribes." [154]

Jesus is seeking those who accept His call to be a humble servant. For, "just so, the Son of Man did not come to be served, but to serve and to give his life as a ransom for many." [155] For as St. Paul taught, "do nothing out of selfishness or out of vainglory; rather, humbly regard others as more important than yourselves, each looking out not for his own interests, but everyone for those of others." [156] Jesus is

---

[152] Matthew 5:39

[153] Matthew 5:41-42

[154] Matthew 7:28-29

[155] Matthew 20:28

calling for us to be like Him, to love like He loved. We must find a means to bring forth the love of Christ for the benefit of all. We must act in selflessness for the benefit of our neighbor. Our deed beads can be the chain that binds us to the love and humility of our Savior. We can feed the hungry or give comfort to those in pain. We can show compassion to those who feel darkness and despair. We can relieve anxiety for those lacking in trust and hope in our Lord. These are the gifts He asks us to carry to the least of His brothers and sisters. He is asking us to show kindness where there could be anger. He is asking us to show patience where there could be ridicule. Just as Saint Francis sought to be the channel of Jesus' love, we are to be an instrument of His hope and of His peace. Practice can make perfect when the call is for an act of humility in the name of Jesus.

There is a litany of occasions to practice humility where Christ presents himself to us in both the least and in the greatest. Where there is poverty or homelessness, offer some financial recompense. Where you encounter the elderly, offer assistance. Cease to argue a point, avoid embarrassing another, and relinquish and let go of your grievances. At all costs, avoid both piling on against the name of another or the opportunity to engage in gossip. Do not criticize and do not judge. Temper your ambition and douse the destructive flames of vanity and pride. Divert any focus or attention that falls upon you and seek to change the "me" to "we" (or he or she). Listen when you are want to talk and offer tenderness and compassion where you find despair. Become an instrument of peace and tranquility on your walk in faith.

"Amen, I say to you, unless you turn and become like children, you will not enter the kingdom of heaven. Whoever humbles himself like this child is the greatest in the kingdom of heaven." [157] Little ways are His ways. In humility, while you are leading those in need to the footstool of the Lord, you will also be leading yourself. In your earnestness for others, you will find the comfort of the Most High. As you clothe others with love and compassion, you will also "clothe yourselves with humility in your dealings with one another, for: 'God opposes the proud but bestows favor on the humble.' So humble yourselves under the mighty hand of God, that he might exalt you in due time." [158]

---

[156] Philippians 2:3-4

[157] Matthew 18:3-4

[158] 1 Peter 5:5-6

Below is a beautiful story relayed by Mike Palmer, a Holy Cross Seminarian: [159]

There was once a man and his friend who decided to go on a long hiking trip through the mountains. One day they came upon a river which, though not very wide, was deep and had a strong current which made it difficult to swim across. Although both men were excellent swimmers, the first man asked his friend to help him build a simple but sturdy log bridge across the river. The two men worked in near-silence for hours. Finally, once the bridge was finished and they had resumed their journey, the second man asked the first, "Why did we have to stop and build that bridge? We could have easily swum across on our own." His friend replied, "I know—I built the bridge for those coming after us who can't."

On our journey in life, we are called to more than that which is readily and easily in front of us. We are called to bigger and greater actions, actions that are found in littleness and simplicity. We are called to forego our needs and seek the needs of our neighbor. We are asked to share in the graces we have received, and do all that we can to provide loving support to our fellow brothers and sisters who are on their walk in faith. Humility is His call to our sanctity. "When you seek me with all your heart, you will find me with you, says the Lord." [160]

With each act of humility, draw forward a bead on your strand of deed beads.

[159] https://www.facebook.com/groups/domo.ni.ekelesia/permalink/1461936477206089
[160] Jeremiah 29:13-14

Contemplate:

1. Do I act in littleness, am I humble? If so, when?

2. To allow Jesus to increase in my life, what are some of the things I can strive to decrease in my life?

3. What are some specific things I can do to increase my practice of humility?

4. Which saint(s) do I admire for their humility and why?

Cross, toil, tribulation:

such will be your lot as long

as you live. That was the way

Christ followed, and the disciple

is not above his Master [161]

BEAD FIVE

Suffer with Him

One of the more difficult concepts to accept in the realm of our relationship as Man with Creator, is the call to humbly accept "suffering" on our walk in faith. Our walk in littleness is a walk towards sanctity. As Our Father is perfect, so too must we be perfect to enjoy the beatific vision, the gift of an eternal presence before the face of the Divine. Holiness, or complete sanctity, is thus a requirement for a life of eternal salvation. The holiness that we seek, yet likely that we fail to achieve in this life, will manifest itself in the heavenly kingdom, if we are so called to enjoy this eternal gift. Purgatory is where we must bridge the fullness of sanctity that remains from our earthly life to that of our heavenly life. That which we can accomplish in this life, in holiness, is a walk in faith with our Savior. Our earthly suffering is a prelude to that which may be asked of us by Our Lord, as we suffer the purification of Purgatory in preparation for the joyous greeting to enter the Heavenly Kingdom. Thus, suffering is a bitter reality of the road to eternal salvation and one that we are called to accept and endure. As Pope Benedict XVI wrote, "In his messengers Christ himself still suffers, still hangs on the Cross. And yet he is risen, irrevocably risen. Although Jesus' messenger in this world [us] is still living the story of Jesus' suffering, the splendor of the Resurrection shines through, and it brings a joy, a 'blessedness,' greater than the happiness he could formerly have experienced on worldly paths." [162]

From man's sinfulness, it is clear that our ways are not God's ways. God's ways are perfect. The Heavenly King is an essence of purity and love that we cannot fully comprehend nor fully emulate in even the remotest sense. Yet, this is the mystery of faith. Our love of God is an inherent longing for the Glorious King whom we can only know by the limits of our understanding and, more importantly, by that which He has revealed to us. What God has revealed to us, through His Son Jesus Christ, is that we are all called to suffer for the greater glory of ourselves, others, and to the call of the Creator. Although Christ could have come before us

[161] St. JoseMaria Escriva. *The Way, Furrow, the Forge,* (Scepter Publishing, New York, New York) 1988, the Way verse 699, pg. 175.

[162] Joseph Ratzinger, Pope Benedict XVI. *Jesus of Nazareth,* (Doubleday, New York, New York) 2007, pg.72-73.

as a king of our understanding and expectation, He did not! He did not come to conquer through our understanding and expectation of power and might, but rather to conquer through littleness and sacrifice. The most astounding concept that we all take for granted is that the most powerful entity in the universe, laid Himself down to be tortured, scourged, crucified and killed by His very subjects, by His creation! Why? Again, in part the mystery of our faith and the ways of our Creator. Yet He tells us, he teaches us, that this is the way, it is His way, for us to reach His Heavenly Home, to live in eternal unity in a perfect love which we know not of in this world.

FAITH can be simply summarized as Forgo All, I Trust in Him or as St. Paul instructs that faith is "the realization of what is hoped for, the evidence of things not seen". [163] Our belief in Christ, our faith, first requires a trust that He is the Way, He is the Truth, and He is the Life. In trust, our actions should align themselves with that which the Master has taught and asked of us. Even those who had the joy and privilege of living with Him on a daily basis, His disciples, did not fully understand His ways. Repeatedly, as Jesus taught them, the disciples failed to fully see His message and failed to fully understand His love and His ways. They are not our ways, and they were not the ways of the disciples. Yet this was the infancy of our faith. Listening and observing and seeking to understand. This is our faith today and the faith that became of the disciples following His death and resurrection, and His coming upon them and amongst them as the Spirit of Holiness. "Then an argument broke out among them about which of them should be regarded as the greatest. He said to them, 'The kings of the Gentiles lord it over them and those in authority over them are addressed as 'Benefactors'; but among you it shall not be so. Rather, let the greatest among you be as the youngest, and the leader as the servant. For who is greater: the one seated at table or the one who serves? Is it not the one seated at table? I am among you as the one who serves.'" [164] These were the seeds of instruction Christ continued to sow for the leaders of His Infant Church. In His suffering, the realization of all that He was and that which He came to achieve, became manifested before them. Now His words "whoever does not carry his own cross and come after me cannot be my disciple" [165] became realized. He went on further to instruct: "If anyone wishes to come after me, he must deny himself and take up his cross daily and follow

---

[163] Hebrews 11:1

[164] Luke 22:24-27

me. For whoever wishes to save his life will lose it, but whoever loses his life for my sake will save it." [166] Thus, to be a disciple of Christ, to grow in sanctity in our walk towards holiness, we must pick up our cross and carry it. We must accept suffering and sacrifice for His sake, whether for our own eternal benefit or that of our brother or sister.

Christ's suffering was intense and it was real. We are told and we believe that His anguish and His agony in the garden were beyond that which we will come to know in our lifetime. For, He fully and deeply understood the inherent imperfection of fallen man, our sinfulness, and the tendency and consistency of Mankind to turn its back on The Father. He fully and deeply understood the pain and injustice we would continue to direct towards the Creator. He fully and deeply understood the sinfulness of our ways and our inclination to choose evil over good. And despite all our iniquities, He fully and deeply understood what was asked of Him, to humbly accept suffering and death for our reconciliation before His Father. Jesus awaited His executioners in prayer in the Garden of Gethsemane and "He was in such agony and he prayed so fervently that His sweat became like drops of blood falling on the ground." [154] Jesus was engulfed in His agony yet accepted it willingly. "Christ also suffered for you, leaving you an example that you should follow in His footsteps. 'He committed no sin, and no deceit was found in His mouth.' When he was insulted, he returned no insult; when he suffered, he did not threaten; instead, he handed himself over." [168]

Following His arrest in the garden, the rocky and difficult walk to the House of Caiaphas, the High Priest, would be through the Kidron Valley, a walk of less than a mile. He knew the torment and mockery that awaited Him at the house of the High Priest, located only several yards from where He spent the Last Supper with His Disciples just hours before, but now what would seem like an eternity of time. Before His accusers He was quiet and humble, for His ways were not their ways, and His truth was not their truth. "They spat in His face and struck Him, while some slapped Him." [169] In response to their demands, Jesus declared

---

[165] Luke 14:27

[166] Luke 9:23-24

[167] Luke 22:44

[168] 1 Peter 2:21-24

[169] Matthew 26:67

His truth, that He was indeed the Son of Man, yet He also knew and stated so, that "If I tell you, you will not believe, and if I question, you will not respond." [170] The fury of the council of elders was in full force, as was the agony of the Divine, our Suffering Servant.

His pain and torment grew to even higher summits when passed over to the hands of the regional governor, Pontius Pilate. Pilate would inherit infamy of a magnitude he knew not of when he sought his position as local leader. He knew not the truth that stood before him. Upon Pilate's inquisition of the King, Jesus proclaimed that "Everyone who belongs to the truth listens to my voice." [171] Yet, Pilate did not comprehend the significance of this prisoner and all that He was as is so succinctly revealed in Pilate's retort, "What is truth?" [172] Pilates' sentence of a scourging at the pillar and later, death by crucifixion sought to fulfill the prophecy of centuries before: "Yet it was our infirmities that he bore, our sufferings that he endured, while we thought of him as stricken, as one smitten by God and afflicted, but he was pierced for our offenses, crushed for our sins, upon him was the chastisement that makes us whole, by his stripes we were healed. We had all gone astray like sheep, each following his own way; but the lord laid upon him the guilt of us all." [173]

The scourging was a most brutal of Roman punishments. The Romans, who were experts at torturing their prisoners to a point just shy of death, found delight in the painful folly of their prey, our Lord and Savior. Chained to a column and muted as is the silence of the lamb, He received their wrath and accepted their blows. Scientists affirm that the Man of the Shroud, the miracle residing in Turin, received more than one hundred lashings with an instrument in cruelty designed at its terminus to divide its pain in multiples. The utensil's (the Flagrum) sole purpose was to efficiently brand a man with human stripes and was further split at its end with weights and claws that achieved a consistent outcome. His flesh became torn, His blood was spilled. The Man of the Shroud, whom most accept was Our Beloved, bore wounds in excess of a thousand. This is our King, the One who was prepared to win our freedom and offer us eternity. He was the sacrifice presented before His Father, for the sake and salvation of all. The cry of mankind

---

[170] Luke 22:67-68

[171] John 18:37

rang loudly in the silence of His Sacred Heart. Although by Jewish custom one could receive not more than 39 lashings, as 40 became the unthinkable, Our Lord was given to those who cared not for Him, and could see not the truth that He was and still remains.

His day was not at its end yet, as the weight of the cross still need to lay upon His shoulders, the nails to meet their foe. The King remained to be crowned by Man before His ascent to His earthly throne on Calvary. The thorns came to their rest upon the brow of our Lord, injecting their mark and madness aligned with the halo of our Savior. The pain would be excruciating as his sensitivities were inflamed. Yet, this was Our King, this was the reign that was His, this was the throne He accepted for the benefit of all. Christ lifted His cross and began His walk. Step by step, little way by little way, Our Lord showed us the way, His way. For our sinfulness, this was the only escape, the only road to salvation. Thus, as any great King would do, He led the way, He was the first, He carried the cross. "Every action done so as to cling to God in communion of holiness, and thus achieve blessedness, is a true sacrifice." [174] This was the Lamb who had come to take away the sins of the world. He was poked and prodded. He was beaten and torn. With His crown adorned, he carried his royal staff, the cross upon His shoulders. He carried the sinful weight of the world. In His exhaustion, He kissed the Via Dolorosa upon His multiple falls, assured of His impact by the burden He carried. Bloodied and brutalized, He continued to rise and ascend to His throne.

Atop the mount of Calvary, He was now to be lifted up as a sacrifice for all. Muted and in silence, He embraced His Cross. He extended His Hands, He laid bare His feet. Blow by blow, the iron drove through His flesh to pin Him to the tree. Like a notice tacked to a wall, with no remorse or forethought by His executioners, Our Christ, the Son of the Creator, was nailed to the Cross and raised upright for all the world to see. His precious blood ran down the wood and sweetened the earth below. His pain brought jeers, His silence brought mockery. Breath by labored breath, as His three long agonizing hours wore on, He still had things to say, He still had a world to teach, He still had His way to impart. From His Gibbet

---

[172] John 18:38

[173] Isaiah 53:4-6

[174] *CCC* 2099, pg. 509 as St. Augustine, De civ. Dei 10, 6, J.P. Migne, ed., Patrologia Latina (Paris: 1841-1855) 41, 283.

high above, Jesus whispered His last, the following for the world to hear:

- ***"Father, forgive them, for they do not know what they do"*** [175]

Jesus' mercy was great, His forgiveness was for all.

- ***"Truly, I say to you, today you will be with me in Paradise"*** [176]

Jesus shows His divinity and reveals what He has taught, that the Kingdom of Heaven is open to all who accept His truth and accept His way.

- ***"Woman, this is your son." To John, "This is your mother."*** [177]

As Simeon's prophecy to the Blessed Mother comes to greet her, that a sword will pierce her soul,[178] Jesus reaches out His embrace to His mother and offers her as the new Eve for all the world to love. To His trusted disciple, the only one who remained at His side, Jesus gives all the world His mother.

- ***"My God, my God, why have you forsaken me?"*** [179]

His suffering was at its peak. As He came to redeem the world, to reconcile all mankind by His sacrifice on the cross, He felt not the comfort of His Father. He also exclaimed the introductory words of Psalm 22 which goes on to profess the truth at hand, "they have pierced my hands and my feet, they have numbered all my bones". [180] The Psalm continued: "they divide my garments among them, and for my vesture they cast lots". [181]

- ***"I thirst"*** [182]

Our Lord was a man. His pain was real; His suffering was intense. Christ felt the pangs of His sentence. The torture, scourging and crucifixion left our Lord with exceeding thirst, yet His thirst would only be fully quenched when He expired His last and brought forth the fullness of His sacrifice for the good of the many. His thirst has a deeper and more profound meaning however. The Passover meal

---

[175] Luke 23:34

[176] Luke 23:43

[177] John 19:26-27

[178] Luke 2:35

[179] Matthew 27:46; Mark 15:34

[180] Psalm 22:17-18

[181] Psalm 22:19

had a ritual in which four cups of wine were drunk during the evening. The Last Supper is the fulfillment of the Passover meal as the true Lamb of God, Jesus, was now present to partake and become the centerpiece of the religious celebration and to fulfill in reality the promises of the Old Covenant. In the Passover celebration, the blood of the lamb was to be spread across the doorpost in order to avoid the wrath of the Angel of Death and hence bring new life to all those acting in accordance with God's will and His law. Additionally, the Passover lamb was to become the centerpiece of the meal. In the Last Supper, new life was gained by the true sacrifice of Christ, the Lamb of God. Partaking in His Body and Blood fulfilled what the Passover foreshadowed. [183]

At the Last Supper, the gospels record that Jesus only consumed three cups of wine and left the ritual open-ended when he told His Disciples who fully understood the ritualistic requirements of the four cups of the Passover meal, that He would not drink of the fruit of the vine again until the kingdom of God was at hand. [184] After many hours of agony and pain, in a subtle yet significant way, the Lamb announced to all His intent to bring to fulfillment the new life of the Passover. Upon uttering His "thirst", he receives a sponge full of vinegar from the soldiers on hyssop (which coincidently is how ritualistically the blood of the lamb is to be spread across the doorpost at the feast of Passover). Here He receives the fourth and final cup, offering new life to all as he then proclaims... [185]

- *"It is finished"* [186]

Christ had come and lived among us, for all the world to come to see and know the love of the Father. He was a Divine gift from above, that was ridiculed and rejected. Yet, by the glory of God, His suffering had now come to its end, an end that in Heaven would now cease to exist for all eternity.

- *"Father, into your hands I commend my spirit"* [187]

Oh the joy their divine embrace must have been, Father and Son! Sadly, our sin

---

[182] John 19:28

[183] Thomas Allen et al. *A Guide to the Passion, 100 Questions About "The Passion of The Christ"*, (Ascension Press, West Chester, PA) 2004.

[184] Luke 22:18

[185] Scott Hahn. *The Fourth Cup*, (Lighthouse Catholic Media).

[186] John 19:30

[187] Luke 23:46

had rejected Our God. It was by Jesus' sacrifice that we could come to know of the fullness of His love for us and the gift of salvation that He could still offer to us. In the beginning, Our Father in Heaven rested on the seventh day and saw that all was good, "Thus the heavens and the earth and all their array were completed. Since on the seventh day God was finished with the work he had been doing, he rested on the seventh day from all the work he had undertaken." [188] So too for His Son, He had come and completed His work, to save all Man, and after His seventh statement from His cross, He too could now rest and all would be good.

Thus the suffering of the Divine is a mystery indeed. Yet, it is the gift we have been given from above. "The cross is the unique sacrifice of Christ, the 'one mediator between God and men'." [189] But because in His incarnate divine person He has in some way united himself to every man, 'the possibility of being made partners, in a way known to God, in the paschal mystery' is offered to all men." [190] As was taught by the Council of Trent in the 16th Century, the unique character of Jesus' sacrifice became the source of our eternal salvation. "His most holy Passion on the wood of the cross merited justification for us." [191]

Christ established His Church on earth through the actions and ministry of His Apostles, to whom He passed the torch, literally, of His Spirit of truth and guidance. "Then there appeared to them tongues as of fire which parted and came to rest upon each one of them. And they were all filled with the Holy Spirit and began to speak in different tongues, as the Spirit enabled them to proclaim." [192] Out of love and trust, His disciples now came to more fully understand all that Jesus was, and all that He instructed. They had now come to fully understand the weight of His words, and the weight of the cross they would now be asked to carry on His behalf, for the sake of all. They now could see the truth and commitment which they all accepted in Jesus' statement: "Whoever wishes to come after me must deny himself, take up his cross, and follow me." [193]

So too, the onus now rests upon us. Jesus has called for us each to "take up

---

[188] Genesis 2:1-3

[189] *CCC* 618

[190] *CCC* 618

[191] *CCC* 617, pg. 160 as Council of Trent: Denzinger-Schonmetzer, *Enchiridion Symbolorum, definitionum et declarationum de rebus fidei et morum* (1965), 1529.

his cross, and follow". Christ has shown us the way and He has proclaimed the truth. "By his passion and death on the cross Christ has given a new meaning to suffering: it can henceforth configure us to him and unite us with his redemptive Passion." [194] Thus, we need to carry our cross; we need to share in the sacrifice that Christ Our Savior bore for the sake of all. Suffering, whilst a mystery in some regard, is an integral part of our faith in Christ. Suffering was an inherent aspect of the way of our Lord, the truth He proclaimed, and the life He offered. His disciples picked up their crosses and so shall we, "for we are God's co-workers". [195]

We are each unique ornaments on God's tree of life. Adorned with an inner beauty, we each must strive to manifest the brilliance God gave each of us, to shine with a luminescence for all to see. In suffering, we willingly open ourselves to God and allow His light to shine before all. Our suffering and sacrifice can thus bring beauty to our lives and to the lives of others. Just as Christ brought salvation to all through His suffering, we too can use suffering to bring about good for the benefit of our brother and for our sister, for our neighbors, for souls in the past or those in the future, and for our enemies. As co-workers of Christ, we can share in His pain and share in the salvation offered to all.

Suffering in our lives can manifest itself in so many ways, from the simple to the profound. We see suffering everyday in the papers, in the news, and in our lives. Suffering can be the loss of a loved one or the sadness that accompanies an illness. Suffering can be seen on the stage of life by tragic loss in natural disasters, in war and in poverty. Oppression and violence can throw suffering and pain to the doorstep of many individual's lives. Sickness and infirmities can bring power to anxiety and helplessness. Economic woes of joblessness and poverty can breed fear and despair. Starvation and death can yield to despondency and disdain. These are a few of the more profound and overt forms of suffering that we will encounter in some manner during our lifetime. These are examples of suffering that all mankind has seen since the Fall of Man, and will continue to experience through to the last. It is a reality of our being, and one we do not experience alone. However, in the throes of such suffering is the time when Christ asks us to

---

[192] Acts 2:3-4

[193] Mark 8:34

[194] *CCC* 1505, pg. 376.

[195] 1 Corinthians 3:9

carry His cross, to share in His pain. Just as Simon the Cyrenian was innocently drawn into the suffering of Christ, to help Him carry His cross, so too does Christ accompany us on our walk in suffering, to help us carry our cross. For "behold, I am with you always" [196] Jesus is there in the silence of our pain, seeking to bring redemption from the suffering in our lives. Accept it and embrace it for the glory of God.

We can embrace suffering in the simple and in the subtle. We can humble ourselves in silence at the insult of another. We can give without reward and we can avoid just recognition. We can offer the discomforts of a simple pain for the benefit of the Father. We can forgo a snack or a meal and thereby not feed our hunger. A fast can bring willful discomfort for the benefit of the sacrifice. These are but a few of the times and manners in which we can open our very soul to the pains of this world, and willingly and lovingly recast them under full embrace for the gifting back to our Father. We can accept the uncomfortable for the good that Christ can allow it to become.

Unknowingly, we may innocently pass by an opportunity to enjoin ourselves to the cross of Christ, for His cross, these crosses, are always there. However, it is how we embrace them and what Christ can do with them that is the beautiful mystery of the ways of our Creator. Such magnificence can be achieved by the willful acceptance of suffering for the greater glory of God. Whether the fruits of the reward are returned in our life or the life of our neighbor, it matters not. We will have chosen to carry His cross and to share in the redemption that is available to all. Recall the beauty and blessedness in the sufferings set forth in Christ's Sermon on the Mount. Blessings abound for the meek, the humble, for those who mourn and for the persecuted. "This intimacy through suffering, when freely chosen, can bring about something exceedingly strange and wonderful: a deep, strong, and unmistakably authentic joy." [197]

So in our pain, let us find joy. As the two disciples felt despair and hopelessness in their sufferings as they walked along the road to Emmaus, they later came to find that their Savior, the Christ, had been with them all along. Christ was walking

---

[196] Matthew 28:20

[197] Peter Kreeft. *Catholic Christianity: A Complete Catechism of Catholic Beliefs Based on the Catechism of the Catholic Church* (Ignatius, 2001).

by their side in their time of despondency; He was hidden from them but was there to alleviate their suffering. After He revealed himself to them through the breaking of the bread, the two disciples later admitted, "Were not our hearts burning within us while he talked with us on the road and opened the Scriptures to us?" [198] Let us come to find the suffering that we can avail ourselves to, whether in the simple or in the profound. Let us willingly accept the difficulties in our lives, and accept the opportunities to suffer in sacrifice for our Lord. For out of our suffering, He will bring eternal joy, just as "when a woman is in labor, she is in anguish because her hour has arrived; but when she has given birth to a child, she no longer remembers the pain because of her joy that a child has been born into the world." [199] Let us suffer with Jesus and help carry the crosses that need to be carried. We can use our deed beads on our road to Calvary to count the ways in which we hoist the cross upon our shoulders and bear the weight for Him.

As we come to use our deed beads to acknowledge and count the ways that sufferings are embraced in our lives, perhaps we can come to view our sufferings in a more beautiful light. Perhaps we can come to understand our sufferings just as we view the clouds of the sky. Just as suffering exists in the lives of man, so too do clouds exist in the blue of the sky. Clouds can be dark and ominous at times, bringing weary weather and torrents of storm. Clouds can be full with a settling fog that obscures our view and the warmth of the sun above. These can be the days and times when suffering is at its peak. Respite and relief from suffering exists as well, and these are the cloudless days when we enjoy the full and sustained brilliance of the sun. At such times, the sky is beautiful and placid, and all is well. However, such a cloudless sky, in all its beautiful blue brilliance, will not last, nor should it, for we too would grow weary over time of a sky that brought not rain to quench our thirst and that of the ground on which we walked. A cloudless blue sky, though beautiful, would breed complacency and a longing to enjoy a parting shadow from above or randomness to the light of our day. It is in the blue heavens above, dotted with each unique and beautiful passing cloud, that we enjoy the greatest fruits of God's ethereal creation. This is when the sky is at its greatest comfort. It is during these typical and common days when the blue sky is adorned with white clouds, in all their novelty. It is during such cloud-dotted

---

[198] Luke 24:32
[199] John 16:21

days that we can come to see a smattering of sufferings and potential crosses for each of us in our day. Each is unique in its own little way. Each can dot our day with an effect on the warmth and light that we experience from above. Each little drifting cloud comes in different shapes and sizes, yet drifts across our lives and is passing and temporary. Through it all however, "the clouds [and suffering] make us see the extra beauty beyond." [200]

Our lives on earth are but a moment in time as compared to an eternal life in heaven. In following Christ's ways, we should be open to sacrifice, accepting of crosses, motivated by burdens, as each is our way to share in His way. Using our deed beads, we can practice acclimation to the many burdens and crosses that come our way. We can accept suffering and embrace sacrifice and count these with our beads as gifts back to our Creator.

As was prayerfully written:

Lord,
Whether it be unfair treatment, fatigue or frustration at work,
A lapse of health, tasks beyond talents, seasons of loneliness,
Bleakness in prayer, the aloofness of friends;
Or whether it be the sadness of our having inflicted any of this on others,
We know that there will be dying to do on our way to You.
But we also know that there is no failure that Your love cannot reverse,
No humiliation You cannot exchange for blessing,
No anger You cannot dissolve,
No routine You cannot transfigure.
All is swallowed up in victory of your Son's cross.
You have nothing but gifts to offer.
In picking up our daily crosses,
Help us to find how even the cross can be borne as a gift. Amen. [201]

---

[200] Don Osgood. *Listening for God's Silent Language*, (1995) pg. 100.

[201] Reverend Andrew Gawrych, CSC; www.holycrosscongregation.org

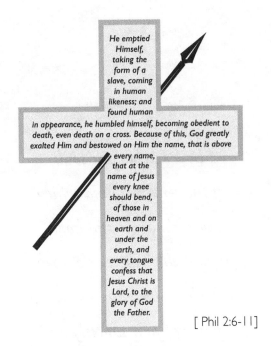

He emptied Himself, taking the form of a slave, coming in human likeness; and found human in appearance, he humbled himself, becoming obedient to death, even death on a cross. Because of this, God greatly exalted Him and bestowed on Him the name, that is above every name, that at the name of Jesus every knee should bend, of those in heaven and on earth and under the earth, and every tongue confess that Jesus Christ is Lord, to the glory of God the Father.

[Phil 2:6-11]

Contemplate:

1. How can I explain the good that can come from suffering and sacrifice?

2. Am I willing to suffer and sacrifice for Christ?

3. How can I ensure that the suffering in my life is used for the Glory of God?

4. What might be some sacrifices that I can make for the Glory of God?

Be a Eucharistic soul!
If the center around which
your thoughts and hopes
turn is the Tabernacle, then,
my child, how abundant the
fruits of your sanctity and
apostolate will be! [202]

BEAD SIX

Adore Christ

"I am with you always" were the parting words of our Lord and Savior as He ascended before His disciples to the throne of His Father's Kingdom. [203]   He came to teach. He came to suffer for our reconciliation before His Father. He returned to His Father, yet He promised to leave us not alone. Our salvation depends on His presence in our lives, both 2000 years ago as well as today. To find eternal rest in the house of our Father, we must allow Jesus to become present in our daily life for He is the Way.

We must seek to make Christ the center of our life, in all that we do, in all that we say, in all that we embody on our walk in faith. We know and understand the Commandments of our Father, yet we find temptation at every turn on the narrow road to Christ. Thus, we cannot and will not achieve salvation on our own. We need the fruits of the Holy Spirit, the guidance of Christ, and the mercy of the Father to avail ourselves of salvation. Jesus revealed the Bread of Life that is available to us, "For the bread of God is that which comes down from heaven and gives life to the world...I am the bread of life; whoever comes to me will never hunger, and whoever believes in me will never thirst." [204]

Allow Jesus to become your spiritual nourishment. Christ became this heavenly sustenance for the lowly simpleton, Sister Maria Faustina Kowalska, when He came to guide and instruct this young polish nun in the 1930s. To this future Saint, Christ revealed the nourishment He provides, the unfathomable gift that is He. Jesus instructed His young pupil, "when you reflect upon what I tell you in the depths of your heart, you profit more than if you had read many books. Oh, if souls would only want to listen to My voice when I am speaking in the depths of their hearts, they would reach the peak of holiness in a short time." [205]   He is the heavenly gift for our salvation. Seek Him. Come to know Christ in all His

---

[202] St. JoseMaria Escriva. *The Way, Furrow, the Forge,* (Scepter Publishing, New York, New York) 1988, the Forge verse 699, pg. 780.

[203] Matthew 28:20

[204] John 6:33-35

[205] Saint Maria Faustina Kowalska. §584, pg. 246.

fullness. The sanctity we seek can be found in the littlest of ways, in silence before our Lord. In quiet, with patience, let the Heavenly Host whisper to our souls and guide us with His grace.

Find a moment, the moment, to be with and before the Lamb of God. In solitude, seek and you will find. Just as Jesus frequently sought solitude from the masses to be before His Father, so too should we seek refuge before our Lord. "Rising very early before dawn, he left and went off to a deserted place, where he prayed." [206] Make an effort to find solitude with the Heavenly King. As Jesus revealed to Saint Faustina, "I desire to bestow My graces upon souls, but they do not want to accept them…they have time for everything, but they have not time to come to Me for graces." [207] Let not your focus be centered on the goods and issues of the world, but rather turn your gaze inward to the Host who is awaiting you. Jesus is there in the tabernacle of your soul, awaiting your knock that He might answer.

Find a moment in the busyness and restlessness of your life to center your focus on the Lamb, to contemplate Our Lord who is there waiting for you. Contemplation is a "gaze of faith, fixed on Jesus". [208] Rest assured that with your focus, the light of the countenance of Christ will illuminate the eyes of your heart, and He will teach you to see all in the light of His truth. [209] Persevere in your efforts for we must pray with hope and trust in our Savior, "I waited, waited for the Lord; who bent down and heard my cry". [210] Do not expect greatness in the moment as we come to expect greatness in our world today. You need not a miracle of locution or grand exaltation. Rather, in silence, in solitude, center your love and trust on the Lord and open the gate for Him that can do all things. Allow the Lord to build you up from the inside out. Step by step, little way by little way, allow the Lamb to purify the pasture.

Seek a dwelling place with the King where you forgo your tendencies toward pride and your focus on self. "Let our masks fall and turn our hearts back to

---

[206] Mark 1:35

[207] Saint Maria Faustina Kowalska. §367, pg. 165.

[208] CCC 2715.

[209] CCC 2715

[210] Psalm 40:2

[211] CCC 2711

the Lord who loves us, so as to hand ourselves over to Him as an offering to be purified and transformed." [211] To do so, requires purity of heart and purity of intention. We must become simple before our Lord to avail ourselves of the gifts of grace He seeks to bestow. We must be childlike in our intentions and in our focus. In seeking to hear the Word of God, we need "the obedience of faith, the unconditional acceptance of a servant, and the loving commitment of a child." [212] As the insightful and articulate Venerable Archbishop Fulton Sheen proclaimed, humble yourself and become like the flute that is empty of air and allow Christ to breathe in His being and make heavenly music through you. [213]

Tuning in to the graces and gifts of our Lord, requires that we tune out the chaos and commotion of our world. He is there, always. "Speak, Lord, for your servant is listening". [214] His message to Saint Faustina was that His gifts were endless, His mercy was limitless, if only we trust in His goodness and seek His compassion. Jesus asks that we find ways to find Him, that we find ways to hear Him. "I desire trust from My creatures. Encourage souls to place great trust in My fathomless mercy. Let the weak, sinful soul have no fear to approach Me, for even if it had more sins than there are grains of sand in the world, all would be drowned in the unmeasurable depths of My mercy." [215] What joy! Salvation does await those who seek Him with a contrite and humble heart. Forgiveness is at hand! Now is the time to seek Him for "I have eternity for punishing [sinners], and so I am prolonging the time of mercy for the sake of [sinners]. But woe to them if they do not recognize this time of My visitation." [216] With childlike humility, through little ways, go to Him and grow in sanctity. Mercy shall be yours.

> Souls that make an appeal to My mercy delight Me. To such souls I grant even more graces than they ask. I cannot punish even the greatest sinner if he makes an appeal to My compassion, but on the contrary, I justify him in My unfathomable and inscrutable mercy. Before I come as a just Judge, I first open wide the door of My mercy. He who refuses to pass through the door of My mercy must pass through the door of My justice. [217]

---

[212] *CCC* 2716.

[213] Archbishop Fulton Sheen. *St. Thérèse: A Treasured Love Story*, (Basilica Press, Irving, Texas) 2007, pg. 156.

[214] 1 Samuel 3:9

[215] Saint Maria Faustina Kowalska. §1059, pg. 399.

[216] Saint Maria Faustina Kowalska. §1160, pg. 424.

[217] Saint Maria Faustina Kowalska. §1146, pg. 420.

As the Father is perfect, so too is His mercy and so too is His justice. Come before the table of the Lord that He might lead you to perfection. He is there and offers an escape from all that weighs us down. He is our bread of life. As a means to move a deed bead for a step towards sanctity, seek Him in Eucharistic Adoration. In the silence and sanctity of the chapel, He awaits you. "So you could not keep watch with me for one hour?" [218] Saint Pope John Paul II guided the flock in this regard, "Let us be generous with our time in going to meet Jesus and ready to make reparation for the great evils of the world. Let your adoration never cease." [219] So too did Blessed Pope Paul IV emphasize the need for all to seek our Savior where he lovingly awaits us, "Christ is reserved in our churches as the spiritual center of the heart of the community, the universal Church and all humanity, since within the veil of the species, Christ is contained, the Invisible Heart of the Church, the Redeemer of the world, the center of all hearts, by Him all things are and of whom we exist." [220]

In quiet time before the bread of life, the Blessed Eucharist, Christ allows us to take refuge. "Tell sinners that I am always waiting for them, that I listen intently to the beating of their heart...when will it beat for me?" [221] He, with open arms, awaits our loving embrace in adoration. His presence is aptly professed in *Our Sunday Visitor* "in speaking of the 'real presence' in the Eucharist we are recalling that this is the fullest and most rich presence of Jesus. Jesus is present in many ways by His action, care, and power; but the Eucharist is Jesus. He is totally present wherever the Eucharist is present. He is present with all His humanity and all His divinity." [222] Before Him we can come, how can we refuse His offer before His throne? It is only in the Kingdom of God that the palace is always open for us to approach Him. Adoration before the Host is a princely gift. At our disposal, we can come and be with Him, to give our love, to humbly adore, to seek His refuge. To adore Him is to humble ourselves before Him and to acknowledge God as our Creator and as our Savior. It is here that we can exalt His greatness and find comfort in His mercy. It is in quiet adoration before Him "that you can hear My voice, which is so soft that only recollected souls can hear it." [223] Gather yourself, that you might hear His voice and receive His graces.

[218] Matthew 26:40

[219] Pope St. John Paul II. *Dominicae Cenae.*

[220] Pope Paul VI. *Mysterium Fidei.*

[221] Saint Maria Faustina Kowalska. §1728, pg. 610.

This divine gift of adoration is where we give to Him our love and He gives to us His Divine embrace. Time spent in adoration is rich in reward, for the peace and silence of the moment is therapeutic to the needs of our souls. "How great is the value of conversation with Christ in the Blessed Sacrament, for there is nothing more consoling on earth, nothing more efficacious for advancing along the road of holiness!"[224] God's graces flow forth and are there to enrich our commitment and to expand our efforts. Time before the Lord in quiet and contemplation is therapy to our sinful misery. It is in the moment of silence that He bends to our ear, listen and hear His "Ephphatha!" ("Be opened!").[225] In prayer and adoration, hear the will of the Father. Let Him slowly come to guide you on your narrow path, on your walk in discipleship.

Time spent in adoration is therapeutic to the purification of our souls and the growth in our sanctity. Unite yourself with Him in contemplation of the 5 wounds of Christ, particularly at the hour of three o'clock, the time when the Lamb humbled His divinity in silence at the slaughter. Come to see and feel His wounds. Interiorize the depths of His sacrifice for our salvation. Have you truly pondered the pain, the terror, the sacrifice of both the Father and the Son? We can clearly see the faithfulness and sanctity in Abraham's willingness to sacrifice his son Isaac at the request of the Father. So too, and all the more so, is the sacrifice of the Creator before those He has created. Jesus instructed His humble Faustina of His gift to those who come in adoration:

> My daughter, that as often as you hear the clock strike the third hour, immerse yourself completely in My mercy, adoring and glorifying it; invoke its omnipotence for the whole world, and particularly for poor sinners; for at that moment mercy was opened wide for every soul. In this hour you can obtain everything for yourself and for others for the asking; it was the hour of grace for the whole world—mercy triumphed over justice.... in this hour...step into the chapel for a moment and adore, in the Blessed Sacrament, My Heart, which is full of mercy; and should you be unable to

---

[222] Cardinal Donald W. Wuerl and Thomas Lawler. *Our Sunday Visitor*, Excerpt from "The Gift of Faith, A Question and Answer Version of the Teaching of Christ". 2013, www.osv.com/OSVNewsweekly.

[223] Saint Maria Faustina Kowalska. §1779, pg. 630.

[224] Pope Paul VI. *Mysterium Fidei*.

[225] Mark 7:34

step into the chapel, immerse yourself in prayer there where you happen to be, if only for a very brief instant. [226]

At this hour, at this moment of His abandonment and agony, His wounds pour out His balm for our inequity. He lives this sacrifice each and every day for our benefit, that we might come before Him in sorrow, in love, and in adoration for His gift of self and salvation. "At three o'clock…I will refuse nothing to the soul that makes a request of Me in virtue of My Passion." [218] His unfathomable mercy is ours for the asking. His Divine Mercy is available for all. "For, this is the will of My Father, that everyone who sees the Son and believes in Him may have eternal life, and I shall raise him on the last day." [228]

A commitment to the Adoration of your Lord can be achieved not only in a single visit or a designated hour in Perpetual Adoration before the Holy Eucharist, but also by your persistence in visiting and partaking in the Lamb in the sacrifice of the Mass. The Mass is the center of our salvation. It has been revealed to us that the merits and graces of our Father's blessings await those who make a commitment in love to come and adore Him and contemplate Him in the Mass. To St. Margaret Mary Alacoque, Christ revealed His gifts that await those who propagate devotion to His Sacred Heart and who receive Communion on the First Friday of every month for nine consecutive months. To those who entrust their faith in Him and enjoin their fate to the Sacred Heart of Christ Jesus on these nine consecutive First Fridays, Jesus has promised the following: [229]

- I will give all the necessary graces in this state of life
- I will establish peace in their homes
- I will comfort them in all their afflictions
- I will be their secure refuge in life, and above all, in death
- I will bestow abundant blessings upon all their undertakings
- Sinners shall find in My Heart the source and the infinite ocean of mercy
- Tepid souls shall become fervent
- Fervent souls shall quickly mount to high perfection
- I will bless every place in which an image of My Heart is exposed and honored

---

[226] Saint Maria Faustina Kowalska. §1728, pg. 558.

[227] Saint Maria Faustina Kowalska. §1320, pg. 474.

- I will give to priests the gift of touching the most hardened hearts
- Those who shall promote this devotion shall have their names written in My Heart, never to be effaced
- The all-powerful love of My Heart will grant to all those who shall receive Communion on the First Friday of nine consecutive months the grace of final repentance, they shall not die under My displeasure, nor without receiving their Sacraments; My Heart shall be their assured refuge in that last hour.

Thus, in love for our Creator, in thankfulness for all our Heavenly gifts, we must seek to make Him the center of our life. We must contemplate Him often, in silence, and adore the Heavenly King. We must come before Him in the tabernacle of our souls and in the tabernacle of our chapels, to adore all that He is. "Our communal worship at Mass must go together with our personal worship of Jesus in the Eucharistic adoration in order that our love may be complete." [230]   Saint Pope John Paul II went on to further instruct that "Our essential commitment in life is to preserve and advance constantly in Eucharistic life and Eucharistic piety and to grow spiritually in the climate of the Holy Eucharist." [231]   The path is there before us, with open access to the palace of our Lord. Although the path may be narrow, take a little step forward, to humbly come before our Lord, for He "will guide you always." [232]   It is written, "Can a mother forget an infant, be without tenderness for the child of her womb? Even should she forget, I will never forget you. See, upon the palms of my hands I have written your name." [233]   Remember the words of Blessed Pope Paul VI, "How great is the value of conversation with Christ in the Blessed Sacrament, for there is nothing more consoling on earth, nothing more efficacious for advancing along the road of holiness!" [234]

Use your deed beads to advance your relationship with Christ and to grow in holiness. Count the times that you spend a moment with Christ, be it an hour

---

[228] John 6:40

[229] https://www.ewtn.com/library/CHRIST/PROMISES.TXT

[230] Pope John Paul II. Redemptor Hominis.

[231] Pope John Paul II. Redemptor Hominis.

[232] Isaiah 58:11

[233] Isaiah 49:15-16

[234] Pope Paul VI. Mysterium Fidei.

in adoration before the Blessed Sacrament, in a moment of thanksgiving, or in receiving Christ in the Eucharist at Mass. Allow the hour of 3 pm to become a daily invitation to invoke His mercy and offer thanksgiving for His sacrifice. Count the times that you stop to adore your Heavenly King.

Contemplate:

1. How can I make Jesus a more important part of my life?

2. Am I spending time really listening to Christ?

3. Can I commit to spending time just adoring Christ?

4. Can I commit to Christ's call to unify my prayers with Him at the hour of 3 o'clock each day?

When you see yourself with a dry heart, without knowing what to say, go with confidence to the Virgin Mary. Say to her, "My Mother Immaculate, intercede for me." If you invoke her with faith, she will make you taste in the midst of your dryness the proximity of God.[235]

BEAD SEVEN

Let Mary be your Advocate

Her role was like that of no other human soul. Out of humility and purity, she was invited to participate in the greatness of her God, our Father. She was invited to contribute to His mission for all mankind, a mission that carried with it the burdens of the world and the pain of redemptive suffering. As she was greeted by the angel Gabriel, she accepted a responsibility unlike that carried by any other. She was the New Eve, who said "yes" to her Creator and set forth on the matriarchal role for all time, the Mother for all mankind. "The knot of Eve's disobedience was untied by Mary's obedience: what the virgin Eve bound through her disbelief, Mary loosened by her faith."[236] From her would pass the Word Incarnate and she would henceforth become the "Mother of God" (Theotokos).[237]

Out of glory and goodness, God our Father lowered Himself for our benefit through the acquiescence of His daughter Mary. Her purity and her assent brought forth the Word that we might be redeemed of our inequity and offered the fruits of His mercy. Like any mother, yet bearing a sinless purity and perfection, Mary brought sustenance, enrichment and guidance to the life of her offspring. She was there to nurture and support His every effort. She was a giver of gifts, gifts of herself to the needs of her Son. She offered constant love and support to the trials and pangs of her child. She offered comfort where there was ridicule. She offered tears where there was pain. She offered love where there was abandonment. She was His mother. She was the mother of the Savior of the World. She willingly signed on, with knowledge that she would endure a life of pain at the side of her Son, who would be scourged for our inequities, pierced for our transgressions, crucified for our sinfulness. Just as any mother bears the pains of their child, so too did Mary bear the mystical cross of Christ upon her shoulders on His walk in littleness and humility for the sake of all. She accepted the offer of Our God and became blessed among women. "My soul proclaims the greatness of the Lord; my spirit rejoices in God my savior. For he has looked upon his handmaid's lowliness;

---

[235] St. JoseMaria Escriva. *The Way, Furrow, the Forge*, (Scepter Publishing, New York, New York) 1988, the Furrow verse 695, pg. 461.

[236] *CCC* 494, pg. 124 as St. Irenaeus, Adv. Haeres.3, 22, 4.

[237] *CCC* 495, pg. 125 as Council of Ephesus (431).

behold, from now on will all ages call me blessed." [238] How fortunate we are to have such a beautiful Mother, one who continues to nurture and comfort her children today!

As the Ark of the New Covenant, she who bore the Word made flesh, Mary mothered God's only begotten Son. Thus, just as Christ would honor His mother with perfection as called for in the Fourth Commandment, "Honor Thy Father and Thy Mother", so too must we bring honor to her name. The Church, His Church, has embraced this Commandment and clarified the honor due this remarkable gift to the world, Mary, through the proclamation of official dogmas clarifying her role. The first of four dogmas regarding the Blessed Mother was codified at the Council of Ephesus in 431, called by Pope Celestine. The controversy of the day was finally settled with the rightful title of "Mother of God" hoisted upon the Blessed Mother of our Savior. The Council's proclamation was met by joyous celebration by the throngs that waited in prayerful anticipation for the trumpeting of this rightful royal recognition. In part, supporting the Council's proclamation is the theological principle communication of idioms, that is, Christ has two natures as both man and God; thus whatever is true about either His humanity or His Divinity is shared in the essence of Christ himself. [239] As Mary is the Mother of Christ who is God, so too is Mary the Mother of God for all ages. The Council proclaimed: "Mother of God, not that the nature of the Word or his divinity received the beginning of its existence from the holy Virgin, but that, since the holy body, animated by a rational soul, which the Word of God united to himself according to the hypostasis, was born from her, the Word is said to be born according to the flesh." [240] And thus proclaimed, Mary is the Mother of God.

The Church also proclaims the perpetual virginity of the Blessed Mother. From the beginning, theologians have maintained that Mary's perpetual motherhood to her Heavenly King rightly coincides with the New Eve, the New Ark of the Covenant that is found only in the Holy of Holies. As the Mother of God, she was and is forever pure. Not formally defined as such until the Seventh Century and more fully rejoiced in the proclamations of the Second Vatican Council, the Church celebrates Mary's

---

[238] Luke 1:46-48

[239] Scott Hahn. *Hail, Holy Queen: The Mother of God in the Word of God*, (Doubleday, New York), 2001, pg 99-101.

[240] *CCC* 466, pg. 117 as Council of Ephesus.

commitment to her Son, our Savior, and to us her children, as the Mother of all mankind. The Church maintains that Christ's birth did "not diminish his mother's virginal integrity but sanctified it". [241] As this Woman of purity, God's ultimate human masterpiece shared in God's mission to bring salvation to the doorstep of mankind. Mary walked the walk with her son and lived a life focused on the fulfillment of His mission. As the Church so eloquently teaches, "Mary is a virgin because her virginity is the sign of her faith unadulterated by any doubt, and of her undivided gift of herself to God's will." [242]

Unlike mankind, Mary's redemption occurred at the moment of her conception. The dogma of the Immaculate Conception was proclaimed by Pope Pius IX in 1854, in one of the most beautiful professions of faith and truth regarding our Blessed Mother: "The most Blessed Virgin Mary was, from the first moment of her conception, by a singular grace and privilege of almighty God and by virtue of the merits of Jesus Christ, Savior of the human race, preserved immune from all stain of original sin". [243] God chose Mary above all women to bring forth His only begotten Son, Our Lord Jesus Christ. He did not need Mary, but he chose Mary as the New Ark of the Covenant. The Second Vatican Council elaborates on Mary's lifelong role in purity: "embracing God's salvific will with a full heart and impeded by no sin, she devoted herself totally as a handmaid of the Lord to the person and work of her Son, under him and with him, by the grace of almighty God, serving the mystery of redemption." [244]

And finally, it wasn't until the middle of the 20th Century that Mary's Assumption in to Heaven as full body and soul was declared. On November 1, 1950, Pope Pius XII solemnly declared: "By the authority of our Lord Jesus Christ, of the Blessed Apostles Peter and Paul, and by our own authority, we pronounce, declare, and define it to be a divinely revealed dogma: that the Immaculate Mother of God, the ever Virgin Mary, having completed the course of her earthly life, was assumed body and soul into heavenly glory. [245] The Assumption of Mary completes the earthly sojourn of the handmaid of the Lord as the vessel for the Word becoming

---

[241] Pope Paul VI. *Lumen Gentium*.

[242] *CCC* 506, pg. 127 as *Lumen Gentium*.

[243] Pope Piux IX. *Ineffabilis Deus*.

[244] *Lumen Gentium*.

[245] Constitution *Munificentissimus Deus*, no 44.

Flesh, yet transitions her to her new role as Queen of heaven and earth. St. John the Evangelist gives us a glimpse of the role of Queen that her Son afforded her, "Then God's temple in heaven was opened, and the ark of his covenant could be seen in the temple…A great sign appeared in the sky, a woman clothed with the sun, with the moon under her feet, and on her head a crown of twelve stars." [246]

As the Heavenly Queen, Mary could now turn her attention to doing the work of her Son for the advocacy of mankind. As Pope Paul VI declared, "We believe that the Holy Mother of God, the new Eve, Mother of the Church, continues in heaven to exercise her maternal role on behalf of the members of Christ." [247] Her role is multifaceted and enduring. The Second Vatican Council further clarified that "this motherhood of Mary in the order of grace continues uninterruptedly from the consent which she loyally gave at the Annunciation and which she sustained without wavering beneath the cross, until the eternal fulfillment of all the elect. Taken up to heaven she did not lay aside this saving office, but by her manifold intercession continues to bring us the gifts of eternal salvation…Therefore the blessed Virgin is invoked in the Church under the titles of Advocate, Helper, Benefactress and Mediatrix." [238] We see these roles come to life through the testimonials of many chosen souls be they saint or simpleton.

From the cross, Christ gave the world His mother, "Behold, your mother." [249] As all mothers have the rare ability to nurture and guide their brood, so too is the Heavenly Queen prepared to bring guidance and advocacy for all mankind, leading us to the footstool of her Son. As was revealed by Christ to the Venerable Mary of Agreda [circa 1656], "I desire to make known to mortals how much intercession of her [Mary] is worth, who brought restoration of life by giving mortal existence to the immortal God…I wish to make known to them much of that, which according to my high judgment is still hidden concerning the Mother of the Word." [250] Christ further extolled, "I have not revealed these mysteries in the primitive Church, because they are so great, that the faithful would have been lost in the contemplation and admiration of them at a time when it was more necessary to establish firmly

[246] Rev 11:19-12:1

[247] CCC 975, pg. 254 as Paul VI, Credo of the People of God §15.

[248] Lumen Gentium.

[249] John 19:27

[250] Venerable Mary of Agreda. The Mystical City of God, (Tan Books, Charlotte, North Carolina) 2008, pg. 8.

the law of grace and of the Gospel." [251] Over the course of many centuries, Christ has continued to give us His mother to love us and to lead us…to Him.

Apparitions of the Blessed Mother have occurred at various times in our history over the last many centuries. On certain occasions, after careful review and investigation by the Catholic Church, we have received a statement of approval from the Vatican that the events and characterization of such are truthful, factual, and most importantly, consistent with the teachings of the Church. In each of these unique instances, we are free to accept the apparition of the Blessed Mother as truthful, yet we are not required to believe in this meeting with Mary. There are many accepted apparitions of the Heavenly Queen, all directing us in some way or another to her Son.

In the year 1531, a humble peasant named Juan Diego encountered a beautiful, celestial woman while walking on a journey on Tepayac Hill in what is now the area of Mexico City, Mexico. She greeted the shy and fearful Juan as the ever-virgin Mary, Mother of the true God. Adorned in a gown of crimson and gold, with a blue star-spangled mantle over her dress, she stood before him awash in rays of light, with the moon about her feet. She told Juan that she wanted a church built upon the very location of her appearance where she would bring joyful compassion to the needs of all the local people who bring her their sorrows upon this spot. She chastened Juan to deliver this message to the local Bishop and to announce all that he had seen and heard. Upon meeting the Bishop and revealing his story and the call of the beautiful woman, the Bishop was inquisitively intrigued yet unmoved. On a subsequent visit by Juan Diego, at the prodding of the Blessed Mother, the Bishop sought confirmation of Juan's tale by a sign from this woman on the mountain. Juan was soon met by the woman again, who appealing to the Bishop's call for a sign, directed Juan to the top of the hill to retrieve foreign flowers that he would find growing in the soil of Tepayac Hill. Indeed, Juan found beautiful Castilian roses, growing in magnificent glory. Juan retrieved the beautiful yellow roses and gathered them in his tilma that he wore about his shoulders. Upon delivering these then to the Bishop, Juan let fall the beautiful roses for the Bishop, and all those present, to see the sign of the Lady. [252]

---

[251] Venerable Mary of Agreda, pg. 8.

[252] http://catholicism.org/brmichael-guadalupe.html

The beauty lies not in the wonderful array of roses, but in the miraculous impression of the Woman Clothed with the Sun that was imprinted upon the inside of the tilma of Juan Diego. This divine imprint revealed the beauty and grace of the Heavenly Queen who had come seeking that a church be built for the conversion of sinners and the consolation of sorrows. Before this image of the Blessed Mother came a multitude of area Aztecs, all seeking to gaze upon Theotokos, the God-bearer, as the Virgin of the tilma was adorned in beauty and bearing within her Divine Son. Word soon spread about the miracle at Tepayac and there followed the conversion of more than 8 million pagan Aztecs. This massive conversion to the call of Christ continues even through today, as an estimated seven million pilgrims flock each year to the Basilica of Our Lady of Guadalupe on the Hill of Tepayac, all brought before the Lord through the actions of His mother. Our Lady of Guadalupe is there waiting, with the beautiful tilma preserved without loss, for all the world to see.

The modern era of Marian apparitions arose in 1830 in Paris at the convent of the Sisters of Charity. It is here that the humble novice, Catherine Laboure, received an apparition of the Blessed Mother adorned in splendor with rays of light emanating from her hands while she stood upon and crushed the head of the serpent. Mary asked Sister Catherine to have a medal cast with this very apparition of the Blessed Mother, adorned with the inscription, "O Mary Conceived without sin, pray for us who have recourse to thee." The reverse of the medal was to carry the emblem of the cross atop the letter M, beneath which lie two hearts, one crowned with thorns and one bearing a piercing by a sword. The rays emanating from her hands represent the graces Mary bestows upon all who seek her intercession before her Heavenly Son. Over time, the medal has become known as the "Miraculous Medal" as an untold countless number of miracles has occurred amongst the millions who came to wear the medal at Mary's request. In one case in a classroom of 30 girls, all sought the intercession and protection of Mary through their wearing of the medal, except for the cholera that befell the one student who remained indignant. Her relief only came upon her wearing the Miraculous Medal. [253] Even beyond the multitude of miracles attributed to the wearing of this medal, the medal also contributed significantly to the dogma of Mary's Immaculate Conception which ultimately was proclaimed in 1854.

---

[253] Fr. Edward O'Connor. *Marian Apparitions Today, Why So Many?* (Queenship Publishing, California), 1996.

[www.cammonline.org]

This particular dogma bore great fruit in the apparition of Mary to the child Bernadette in 1858 in the most well-known Marian apparition occurring in Lourdes, France. It is here that the uneducated child Bernadette was able to recount the beauty in the Lady she beheld in vision and the name by which this Lady sought to be known, "I am the Immaculate Conception". [254] Mary appeared to little Bernadette in a grotto where she was gathering wood. Mary's proclamation of her Heavenly title of the Immaculate Conception bore great confirmation to this recently announced dogma first pronounced in Rome just four years earlier. Bernadette was a sickly impoverished child living in a town nestled in the Pyrenees Mountains. She was graced with the apparition of Mary on 18 different occasions, each time the Lady humbly and solemnly appeared adorned in a white gown with a blue sash. Our Lady requested that a chapel be built on the site of their meeting underneath which lie a miraculous spring of water that first trickled forth upon Mary's urging of Bernadette to dig in the mud. Mary's fountain has brought forth a multitude of miracles for the thousands of pilgrims who have come to participate in Mary's meeting. Mary left Bernadette with gospel messages of love, prayer and meditations on the rosary. This great apparition has stood firm throughout the years drawing the faithful into the fold of Mary's mantle. [255]

In May of 1917 a great apparition of a Beautiful Lady befell three young children while tending sheep in the fields of Fatima, Portugal. This magnificent flash of light occurred in a field known as Cova da Iria to young Lucia dos Santos, eight years

[254] https://catholicismpure.wordpress.com/2013/11/30/i-am-the-immaculate-conception-our-lady-told-st-bernadette/

[255] http://www.catholicnewsagency.com/resources/mary/popular-marian-devotions/our-lady-of-lourdes/

old, and her two cousins Francisco (7) and his sister Jacinta (5). For approximately two years prior to the coming of this Beautiful Lady, the three children were routinely visited by a celestial being who introduced himself as the Angel of Peace and who prepared the children for her introduction. The Lady first appeared to the children on the 13th of May and again on the 13th day of 6 subsequent months. Each time the Beautiful Lady advocated the perpetuation of the rosary and prayer to the Father in Heaven. On the second visit, the Beautiful Lady taught the children the following prayer that was to be added to each decade of the rosary:

Oh My Jesus, forgive us our sins, save us from the fires of hell,
Lead all souls to heaven, especially those in most need of thy mercy

Mary imparted knowledge to the children regarding the love of God and the mysteries of the Holy Trinity. She imparted three secrets to the children, in the first of which she stated:

"I promise salvation to those who embrace devotion to my
Immaculate Heart. Their souls will be loved by God as flowers
placed by me to adorn His throne. These souls will suffer a
great deal but I will never leave them. My Immaculate Heart
will be their refuge, the way that will lead them to God."

News of this strange event was growing and a multitude of townspeople began to congregate on each 13th day of the month to hear what news was brought to the children, for only they received the grace of the vision of Mary. The visionaries endured persecution and temporary imprisonment by the unbelievers in town as they answered Mary's call for them to endure suffering for the sake of sinners. On the final apparition in October, Mary had promised a great sign for all to behold, that all present might have faith in her truth and attend to her call for prayers for sinners. The Beautiful Lady was true to her word, and on October 13th, 1917, over 50,000 people awaited her visit in the Cova da Iria. While standing in pouring rain, the throng of people observed the sun dancing in the sky, hurling towards earth and then quickly again seating itself back in its place. Many believed this was the end of the world only to then feel the greatness of God when the sun returned to its resting place. This magnificent miracle was witnessed by tens of thousands, both at the Cova and in the surrounding countryside. The miraculous vision was described in the newspapers and brought peace and faith to many of the unbelievers. The hand of God was visible in Mary's apparition and Fatima remains today one of the most widely witnessed miracles and a place of fruitful pilgrimage for the faithful. The parting gift to all those who witnessed this celestial dance in the pouring rain was the miracle of finding that their clothes were completely dry following the vision.

The above noted apparitions are just a few of the numerous interactions of the Blessed Mother with her children. God's gift of these encounters has brought inspiration, peace and renewed faith in the call of the Father for all to gather at his throne. Mary continues to dedicate her every moment to the request of the Father and to bringing children to her son Jesus. The Catholic Church has dedicated significant time and effort to fully understand and document these apparitions, and where validated in faith and in fact, the Church has promulgated the truth of Mary's visit and endorsed belief in the apparition for the faithful. The Church does not require belief in the approved apparitions of Mary, but encourages its study and understanding and finds the apparitions as gifts of God's grace for the faithful who can benefit in their belief. Although the Catholic Church may assess and investigate ongoing apparitions that are occurring even today, the Church will not render a final verdict on the veracity of the appearance until the apparition has come to a conclusion. Thus, such apparitions that some believe to be occurring today offer an opportunity for ongoing assessment and understanding by the faithful.

By the order of grace first presented to Mary at the visitation of the Angel Gabriel sent from on High to present day today, Mary's mission is clear: to bring forth the Word of God made Flesh and to be the advocate of all souls on behalf of her Son. The many apparitions of Mary bear the fruit of her efforts to lead all souls to Him. As our advocate, we need only call upon her to elevate our efforts, to lighten our temptations, to enrich our faith, all by the purity of her love for her Son. As was so eloquently set forth by Pope Paul VI in 1964 through the Second Vatican Council in *Lumen Gentium*, "Mary's function as mother of men in no way obscures or diminishes this unique mediation of Christ, but rather shows its power. But the Blessed Virgin's salutary influence on men...flows forth from the superabundance of the merits of Christ, rests on his mediation, depends entirely on it, and draws all its power from it." [256]

---

[256] *CCC* 970, pg. 253 as *Lumen Gentium*.

Thus, with the countless intercessions by Mary for the well-being of mankind, we must find ways in our day to grasp our deed beads and practice little ways that are demonstrable of our love for our Mother. We must recognize the beauty in her ways and her efforts to lead all souls to heaven. Jesus' love for His mother is perfect and, in accordance with the Fourth Commandment, we should practice veneration of Mary to bring her honor. "Mary is the supreme model of faith (the one who best shows us what it means to believe in God)."[257]

In follow up to her apparition and message at Fatima, the Holy Virgin again appeared to Lucia (later Sister Lucia) on December 10, 1925. At the side of Sister Lucia, Mary appeared with the Child Jesus present on an elevated luminescent cloud. In this apparition she revealed her very heart surrounded by thorns scourging her by the acts of blasphemies and ingratitudes. To Sister Lucia, Mary offered a "little way" for all the world to practice reparation for these painful acts and promised to assist, at the moment of death, with all the graces necessary for salvation, to all those who:[258]

- on the first Saturday of five consecutive months,
- shall confess,
- shall receive Holy Communion,
- shall recite five decades of the Rosary and
- keep Me [Mary] company for fifteen minutes while meditating on the fifteen mysteries of the Rosary,
- with the intention of making reparation to Me [Mary].

The Child Jesus spoke to Sister Lucia to illuminate the significance of dedication to the First Five Saturdays. Jesus proclaimed that there are five types of offenses and blasphemies committed against the Immaculate Heart of Mary for which reparation to her Immaculate Heart is needed:

1. Blasphemies against the Immaculate Conception;

2. Blasphemies against Her Virginity;

3. Blasphemies against Her Divine Maternity, in refusing at the same time to recognize Her as the Mother of men;

[257] Michael E. Gaitley, MIC. 33 Days to Merciful Love: A Do-It-Yourself Retreat in Preparation for Consecration to Divine Mercy (Marian Press, Stockbridge, MA) 2016, pg. 31.

4. The blasphemies of those who publicly seek to sow in the hearts of children, indifference or scorn or even hatred of this Immaculate Mother;

5. The offenses of those who outrage Her directly in Her holy images. Here, my daughter, is the reason why the Immaculate Heart of Mary inspired Me to ask for this little act of reparation. (May 29, 1930)

Thus, we should follow the call of our Mother and our Lord, to devote time to the Blessed Mother on the First Five Saturdays of consecutive months. We can use our deed beads to prompt us along the way, moving a bead for each and every time we bring honor to our Queen or remove a scourging thorn from her heart. Each time we contemplate reparation to her purity, or that we promote the dogma of her Virginity or her Immaculate Conception, we bring honor to our Mother in alignment with the will of her Son, and we can use our beads to traverse the cavern created by the ingratitude of man.

Our deed beads can serve as a tool or reminder for us to pause during our day and reflect on the beauty and purity of our Mother. We can spend time contemplating her pain and her sacrifice for sinners who need calling. We can heed the call of her Son and bring honor to his mother. Catholicdevotions.org provides a listing of beautiful Devotions, Consecrations, Reparations and Litanies we can voice from our hearts for love of the Blessed Mother.

---

[258] http://www.themostholyrosary.com/appendix2.htm

Devotions to the
Immaculate Heart of Mary

My God, I believe, I adore, I trust, and I love Thee; And I beg pardon for those who do not believe, do not adore, do not trust, and do not love Thee.

My God, I believe, I adore, I trust, and I love Thee; And I beg pardon for those who do not believe, do not adore, do not trust, and do not love Thee.

My God, I believe, I adore, I trust, and I love Thee; And I beg pardon for those who do not believe, do not adore, do not trust, and do not love Thee.

O Most Holy Trinity, Father, Son, and Holy Ghost I adore Thee profoundly. I offer Thee the Most Precious Body, Blood, Soul, and Divinity of Jesus Christ, present in tabernacles throughout the world, in reparation for the outrages, sacrileges, and indifference, by which He is offended. By the infinite merits of the Sacred Heart of Jesus, in union with the Immaculate Heart of Mary, I beg the conversion of poor sinners.

O Most Holy Trinity, I adore Thee, My God, my God, I love Thee in the Most Blessed Sacrament.

O my Jesus, it is for love of Thee, in reparation for the offenses committed against the Immaculate Heart of Mary and for the conversion of poor sinners.

Act of Consecration to the Immaculate Heart of Mary

O Immaculate Heart of Mary, Queen of Heaven and Earth, and tender
Mother of men, in accordance with thy ardent wish made known at Fatima,
I consecrate to thy Immaculate Heart myself, my brethren, my country and the whole
human race. Reign over us, Most Holy Mother of God, and teach us how to make
the Heart of Thy Son, Our Lord Jesus Christ reign and triumph in us even as It has
reigned and triumphed in thee. Reign over us, dearest Mother, that we may be thine
in prosperity and in adversity; in joy and in sorrow; in health and in sickness; in life
and in death. O most compassionate Heart of Mary, Queen of Virgins, watch over
our minds and our hearts and preserve them from the deluge of impurity which
thou didst lament so sorrowfully at Fatima. We want to be pure like thee. We want
to atone for the many sins committed against Jesus and thee. We want to call down
upon our country and the whole world the peace of God in justice and charity.

Therefore, we now promise to imitate thy virtues by the practice of a
Christian life without regard to human respect. We resolve to receive Holy Communion
on the First Saturday of every month and to offer thee five
decades of the rosary each day together with our sacrifices in a spirit of
reparation and penance. Amen.

Act of Reparation to the Immaculate Heart of Mary

Most Holy Virgin and our beloved Mother, we listen with grief to the complaints
of the Immaculate Heart, surrounded with the thorns which ungrateful men place
therein at every moment by their blasphemies and ingratitude. Moved by the ardent
desire of loving thee as our Mother and of promoting a true devotion to thy Immaculate
Heart, we prostrate ourselves at thy feet to prove the sorrow we feel for the grief
that men cause thee and to atone by means of our prayers and sacrifices for the
offenses with which men return thy tender love. Obtain for them and for us the
pardon of so many sins. A word from thee will obtain grace and forgiveness for all.
Hasten, O Lady, the conversion of sinners that they may love Jesus and cease to
offend God, already so much offended, and thus avoid eternal punishment. Turn thine
eyes of mercy towards us so that henceforth we may love God with all our heart
while on earth and enjoy Him forever in Heaven. Amen.

Litany of the Immaculate Heart of Mary

Immaculate Heart of Mary, Pray for our dear country.
Immaculate Heart of Mary, Sanctify our clergy.
Immaculate Heart of Mary, Make our Catholics more fervent.
Immaculate Heart of Mary, Guide and inspire those who govern us.
Immaculate Heart of Mary, Cure the sick who confide in thee.
Immaculate Heart of Mary, Console the sorrowful who trust in thee.
Immaculate Heart of Mary, Help those who invoke thine aid.
Immaculate Heart of Mary, Deliver us from all dangers.
Immaculate Heart of Mary, Help us to resist temptation.
Immaculate Heart of Mary, Obtain for us all we lovingly ask of thee.
Immaculate Heart of Mary, Make our family life holy.
Immaculate Heart of Mary, Help those who are dear to us.
Immaculate Heart of Mary, Bring back to the right road our erring brothers.
Immaculate Heart of Mary, Give us back our ancient fervor.
Immaculate Heart of Mary, Obtain for us pardon of our manifold sins and offenses.
Immaculate Heart of Mary, Bring all men to the feet of thy Divine Child.
Immaculate Heart of Mary, Obtain peace for the world.
Let us pray

O God of infinite goodness and mercy, fill our hearts with a great confidence in Thy most holy Mother, whom we invoke under the title of the Immaculate Heart of Mary, and grant us by her most powerful intercession all the graces, spiritual and temporal, which we need. Through Christ our Lord. Amen

Each of the above prayers can assist us in the call of Christ to honor His mother and to comfort the pains she carries for the injustice and the ingratitude of men. We can even go a step beyond walking the row of our deed beads to illuminate the light of the Blessed Mother's graces through the above devotions, by wearing the brown scapular. In the year 1251, on July 16, the Blessed Mother appeared to St. Simon Stock, Superior General of the Carmelite Order, and promised the following to all who wear the brown scapular, the Garment of Grace: [259]

---

[259] http://www.fatima.org/apostolate/pdf/brown_scapular.pdf

[260] http://www.freebrownscapular.com/brown_scapular_history.html

[261] http://www.greenscapular.com/

"Accept this Scapular, it shall be a Sign of Salvation, a Protection in Danger and a Pledge of Peace. Whosoever Dies clothed in this (Scapular) Shall not Suffer Eternal Fire"

"Wear the Scapular devoutly and perseveringly, it is My garment. To be clothed in it means you are continually thinking of Me, and I in turn, am always thinking of you and helping you to secure eternal life." [260]

The Blessed Mother is pleased when Her sons and daughters wear Her Brown Scapular as a mark that they have dedicated themselves to Her service, and are members of the Family of the Mother of God. As a mark of the armor of Mary, those who seek the advocacy of Mary and wear her shield of love will find great strength in the face of temptation. This sign of consecration to and trust in the Holy Mother of God is what she seeks in those who seek little sanctity and humbly trust in her protection. The Church states that the benefits of Mary's proclamation is attached to those who don the Scapular and are enjoined in the confraternity of Carmelites via their prayerful consecration. Pope Benedict XV, the celebrated Pontiff during World War I, granted an indulgence (the remission of time spent in Purgatory for punishment due to sins) of 500 days for each time the Scapular is devoutly kissed.

[bourbonapocalypse.wordpress.com]

The Blessed Mother also introduced the Green Scapular in the year 1839. On the heels of the devotion she established with the Miraculous Medal, our Holy Mother again sought to offer peace and refuge to those who sought her intercession. Through a series of apparitions to Sister Justine Bisqueyburo of the Daughters of Charity, in Paris, the Mother of God appeared holding an Immaculate Heart engulfed in flames in one hand, and in the other, a Green Scapular.[261] Green Scapulars bear a picture of the Blessed Virgin on one side, and her enflamed Immaculate Heart on the other. The scapular bears the inscription, "Immaculate Heart of Mary, pray for us, now and at the hour of our death." Twice approved by Pope Pius IX, in 1863, and again in 1870, the gift of the Green Scapular is the gift itself. It is intended to be given to someone, who is in need of health, conversion, or peace and the scapular requires a simple blessing by a priest. It is to be worn by or carried by the person in need of the Blessed Mother's advocacy and graces. Either the giver or the receiver of the Green Scapular should recite the prayer "Immaculate Heart of Mary, pray for us now and at the hour of our death" on a daily basis. Giving this gift of grace to a friend in need is reason enough for us to move our bead along on our deed bead strand.

[giftshop.wafusa.org]

We have briefly reviewed and seen the gift that Mary is for all mankind. She who bore the Word Incarnate, who brought us the Savior of the World, has remained true to her Son and in accordance with His will, has sought to bring all souls to Heaven's door. We should seek her advocacy before the Heavenly King. We should seek reparation for the sins of man against both her and her Son. We should confidently proclaim ourselves amongst her army of witnesses to faith in Christ, and seek to bring consolation and peace to all our neighbors. We should trust in the intentions of our Mother, in Christ's Mother and embrace the words of Pope Benedict XVI:

> "When Christians of all times and places turn to Mary, they are acting on the spontaneous conviction that Jesus cannot refuse his mother what she asks; and they are relying on the unshakable trust that Mary is also our mother -- a mother who has experienced the greatest of all

sorrows, who feels all our griefs with us and ponders in a maternal way how to overcome them." [262]

Her will is in complete alignment with the will of her Son. What Mary asks, so too her son desires.

Use your deed beads to count the times and ways in which you honor and venerate the Blessed Mother of Christ. She will be an advocate for you before her Son and help you in your *Little Ways to Little Sanctity*.

Contemplate:

1. Do I recognize Mary as the Mother of God and do I fully appreciate the beauty and purity of her life dedicated to her Son, Jesus?

2. Do I believe that I should not worship Mary, but that I should venerate and honor her? Do I understand the difference?

3. How can I increase my relationship with Christ's Mother?

4. Will I call on Mary to be my Advocate before her Son, Jesus?

---

[262] VATICAN CITY (Catholic Online) -- During his apostolic visit to Germany, Pope Benedict XVI led a Marian Vespers celebration on September 23, 2011 at the Wallfahrtskapelle, Etzelsbach, where he prayed the Liturgy of the Hours with the gathered faithful. www.Catechism holic.org 10/16/11.

How beautiful is our Catholic faith!
It provides a solution for all our anxieties;
it gives peace to the mind and fills the
heart with hope.[263]

The perennial vitality of the Catholic
Church ensures that the truth and spirit of
Christ do not become remote from the
different needs of the times.[264]

Our Holy Mother the Church, in a
magnificent outpouring of love, is scattering the
seed of the Gospel throughout the world; from
Rome to the outposts of the earth.
As you help in this work of expansion throughout
the whole world, bring those in the outposts to the
Pope, so that the earth may be one flock and one
Shepherd: one apostolate![265]

BEAD EIGHT

Seek the Treasury of His Church

Christ instituted His Church for the betterment of man and the advancement of holiness for each of her members. The word "Catholic" means "universal" and Christ's institution is for all who are seeking His salvation. Christ is at the center of His Church. The heartbeat of the Church is Christ's heartbeat and the soul of the Church is Christ's soul. As the Alpha and the Omega, Christ is the beginning and the end of His Church. Early Church Fathers described Christ as the light of the Church, there is no other light in the Church but He for "the Church is like the moon, all its light reflected from the sun." [266] To come to know Him more nearly, seek the treasures of His Church.

Gifts abound in the treasury of His Church. It all began some 2000 years ago when Christ asked his closest disciples, "Who do people say that the Son of Man is?" [267] It was upon Simon Peter that the Heavenly Father revealed the truth hidden in Christ's being for Simon proclaimed that Christ was the Messiah, the Son of the Living God. This became a pivotal step in Christ's formation of His Church on earth. "And so I say to you, you are Peter, upon this rock I will build my church, and the gates of the netherworld shall not prevail against it. I will give you the keys of the kingdom of heaven; whatever you bind on earth will be bound in heaven, and whatever you loose on earth will be loosed in heaven." [268] Christ thus laid the cornerstone of His Church in and upon Peter and to him He bequeathed the keys to the kingdom of heaven. Thus, what now was bound through the Church on earth would similarly be bound in heaven. What the Church loosed on earth would similarly be loosed in heaven for the Holy Spirit was its anchor. The power

---

[263] St. JoseMaria Escriva. The Way, Furrow, the Forge, (Scepter Publishing, New York, New York) 1988, the Way verse 582, pg. 144.

[264] St. JoseMaria Escriva. The Way, Furrow, the Forge, (Scepter Publishing, New York, New York) 1988, the Furrow verse 319, pg. 359.

[265] St. JoseMaria Escriva. The Way, Furrow, the Forge, (Scepter Publishing, New York, New York) 1988, the Forge verse 638, pg. 731.

[266] *CCC* 748, pg. 197.

[267] Matthew 16:13

[268] Matthew 16:18-19

to bind and loose is actual for it came from Christ to the Church He instituted. St. Paul instructed the Ephesians about the purity of Christ's Church, just as "Christ loved the church and handed himself over for her to sanctify her, cleansing her by the bath of water with the word, that he might present to himself the church in splendor, without spot or wrinkle or any such thing, that she might be holy and without blemish." [269]   To Peter, and on to his ministers, authority had now been given to forgive sins as Christ forgave sins and to pronounce doctrine as Christ taught doctrine. The foundation laid by Christ does not and will not waver. Thus, His Holy Church came to be and Peter was its anointed shepherd.

God humanized His divinity in His Son Jesus Christ who came to reveal the Way, the Truth and the Life. Jesus reconciled all mankind through His sacrifice on the cross before His Father and at the hands of all man. Jesus' salvation did not end there however. With His ascension into the Kingdom on High, He instituted His Church that His truth might propagate and prepare man for His second coming. On the day of Pentecost, the Holy Spirit descended upon the new ministers of Christ's Church that they might become holy in Christ and that His Church would be sanctified. "The Church, which the Spirit guides in way of all truth and which he unifies in communion and in works of ministry, he both equips and directs with hierarchical and charismatic gifts and adorns with his fruits." [270] Christ planted the seeds of His Church and left His Holy Spirit to provide the nourishment and sustenance to breed life into it that it might grow and be nurtured for all time. Christ is the Shepherd and His Church is "the flock of which God himself foretold he would be the shepherd, and whose sheep, although ruled by human shepherds, are nevertheless continuously led and nourished by Christ himself, the good shepherd and the prince of the herds, who gave his life for his sheep." [271] His Church stands as a beacon of truth for all, that the treasures of Christ might be alive and at hand.

Via the formation of His Church, Christ left behind to His Apostles His truth and His holiness. His words, His truth, and His example gave direction to the Apostles under the ever-present guidance of the Holy Spirit. The Holy Spirit is the giver of everlasting truth and holiness to Christ's Church. "The Holy Spirit, whom Christ

---

[269] Ephesians 5:25-27

[270] *Lumen Gentium.*

[271] *Lumen Gentium.*

the head pours out on his members, builds, animates, and sanctifies the Church. She [the Church] is the sacrament of the Holy Trinity's communion with men." [272] The Apostles thus became the stewards of Christ's Church which was "holy and without blemish". [273] Although directed by sinners, His Church henceforth remained sinless. As the unblemished seedling was now planted by Christ and sustained by the Spirit, it took root in the actions of Christ's Apostles.

Through divine inspiration, Simon Peter inherited the keys to Christ's Church. He now became the source of leadership and inspired truth for the Church in its infancy. "In order that the episcopate itself might be one and undivided, He [Jesus] placed Blessed Peter over the other apostles, and instituted in him a permanent and visible source and foundation of unity of faith and communion." [274] Further to Peter at its head, Vatican II Council affirmed that the apostles and their successors, the bishops, along with Peter and his successors, the Vicars of Christ, govern the house of the living God. The stage had been set by Christ, through Peter and subsequently through the apostles, for His truth to take root. Guided by the Spirit, Peter and his successors have established an unbroken descendancy amongst the Holy See through a line of 266 continuous Pope's leading Christ's flock. Similarly, the apostles have been succeeded by their ministers, the bishops. Fortified in sanctity by the guidance of the Holy Spirit, His church has blossomed and has remained open to all seeking Christ's truth and His treasury.

The twelve accepted Christ's offer to spread His Church. Their training began with Christ on earth, their mission began with Christ's ascension into Heaven. "As the Father has sent me, so I send you." [275] Their ministry became an extension of His Word and His Truth. This ministry was and is available to all for Christ explained to them that "whoever receives you receives me." [276] Guided by the Holy Spirit, the twelve set forth on their mission to evangelize and proclaim the Good News that was Christ. Instituted by Christ, the twelve were "the seeds of the new Israel and the beginning of the sacred hierarchy." [277]

---

[272] *CCC* 747

[273] Ephesians 1:4

[274] *Lumen Gentium.*

[275] John 20:21

[276] Matthew 10:40

[277] *CCC* 877, pg. 232 as Ad Gentes.

With each generation, His Church began to take root and blossom. Early Church Fathers, some of whom were directly taught by the Apostles, gave life and direction to the infant Church and many of their writings, practices, and traditions set the Church on its path for later dogma and doctrine. Historic greats such as Clement of Rome, Ignatius of Antioch and PolyCarp of Smyrna, are names of just a few of the many who began to carry the torch that burned in the original twelve. Oral tradition was the key to learning and teaching, and the practices proclaimed first by the Apostles under the Holy See of Saint Peter, soon became the platform by which Church Fathers proclaimed both orally and in writing the good news of Christ. The ancient writings we find from Church Fathers during the first 500 years of Christ's Church are reflected in the doctrines proclaimed by the Catholic Church today. Historic precedent exists and is traceable to the Church during its infancy.

With established traditions and referenced writings, the Church began to formalize its teachings by the output of arraigned ecumenical councils called and attended by the bishops of the Church. At the first ecumenical council in 325 A.D. at the Council of Nicaea, the Catholic Church began the first promulgation of Church doctrine in the form of the Creed of Nicaea, a creed still recited today at Mass. [278] In 431 A.D. at the Third Ecumenical Council in Ephesus, the Church formalized and professed Mary as the Mother of God. [279] In 451 A.D. at the Fourth Ecumenical Council in Chalcedon, the Church defined the two natures of Christ: Divine and Human. [280]

Not only did the Church begin to grow and flourish under the guidance of the Holy Spirit, but so too did the deposit of faith fortified by the proclamations of the Church Magisterium. The Church hierarchy, in the descendancy of Peter and the Apostles and endowed with the authority of Christ, brought the evolution of truth and Christ's word to the Christian faithful. The Magisterium proclaimed doctrine, established dogma, and taught precepts. As pastors of the Church, the hierarchy set five fundamental precepts to guide the faithful in prayer and moral effort: [281]

---

[278] http://www.newadvent.org/cathen/04423f.htm

[279] http://www.newadvent.org/cathen/04423f.htm

[280] http://www.newadvent.org/cathen/04423f.htm

[281] CCC 2042-2043

[282] Matthew 18:20

1. You shall attend Mass on Sunday and on holy days of obligation and rest from servile labor

2. You shall confess your sins at least once a year

3. You shall receive the sacrament of the Eucharist at least during the Easter season

4. You shall observe the days of fasting and abstinence established by the Church

5. You shall help to provide for the needs of the Church

Doctrinally, following the Council of Trent (1545-1564), the Church taught that the Ten Commandments were obligatory and that all the faithful should follow them. Dogmatically, the Church proclaimed the holy merits of the Blessed Virgin as the Mother of God, her Immaculate Conception, her sanctifying Assumption into Heaven and her Perpetual Virginity. These gifts and these treasures are mere blossoms amongst the flower garden of the Church in terms of its teaching and its Tradition.

Christ's Church had so much more to offer, so much more guidance to bear and light to shine. Through apostolic succession, the same Holy Spirit that was bestowed upon the apostles at Pentecost, remains with the Church's Magisterium today. Guided in holiness, the Church established the Mass and the celebration of the Sunday Eucharist from an early apostolic age. As Christ taught, "where two or three are gathered together in my name there am I in the midst of them". [282] He is there in the species of the Eucharist. He is there in the reading of His Word. The Church established the celebration of the Mass and all its holy content. Sunday became a day of obligation for all the faithful. The Mass is a treasury of holiness for all those seeking to encounter Christ.

A true treasure for all those seeking the guidance and teachings of His Holy Church is found in the *Catechism of the Catholic Church.* In 1985, Saint Pope John Paul II convened a synod of Bishops on the 20th anniversary of the Second Vatican Ecumenical Council to assess how to better avail all the faithful of the fruits and graces of Vatican II. [283] An output of that assembly was the revelation that the Christian faithful sought and desired a more formal compendium of Church doctrine. As a result, Pope John Paul II commissioned twelve Cardinals and Bishops to bring to life such a Catechism. Fortified with the grace of His Holy Church, the *Catechism* was made available for all the faithful in October 1992. In full alignment with the truth found in Sacred Scripture, the Apostolic Tradition and the Church's Magisterium, the *Catechism* illuminates in exquisite detail and ordered arrangement the truth that is professed by and through Christ's Church. It is an authentic text for faithful reference, for learned discourse, and doctrinal stability and understanding. The *Catechism* is a treasured resource directed towards understanding the proclamation of salvation that Christ brings to all through His Church. In his introduction to the Church faithful regarding the beautiful and enriching *Catechism*, Saint Pope John Paul II concluded with the following prayerful sentiment "may the light of the true faith free humanity from the ignorance and slavery of sin in order to lead it to the only freedom worthy of the name: that of life in Jesus Christ under the guidance of the Holy Spirit, here below and in the Kingdom of heaven, in the fullness of the blessed vision of God face to face!" [284]

Think not that the treasury is limited and that it is contained within the walls of the church of man, but rather it exists and lives throughout the Church of Christ. It is also contained in the Communion of Saints who have lived and died over the centuries since the institution of His Church. This body of individuals are members of the Mystical Body of Christ who, by the grace of God, have chosen to persistently follow His Way. These jewels amongst the treasure trove of Christ's Church are representative of the light that shines forth from the Way of Christ. In each individual saint, that luminosity brings forth a different yet unique light. Each saint brings his or her own individuality and shines light on the Way that Christ asks us to walk and they can each help lead us down the narrow path. Like the stars in the heavens, the Communion of Saints bring beauty and individualism, all the while providing light and constancy.

The Communion of Saints is a divine resource for us to find compatibility and to identify with the life they lived and the heavenly salvation they attained. Amongst the saints we will find an immensity of individualism, each offering a life lesson in

[283] *CCC*, pg. 6.
[284] *CCC*, pg. 6.

a different Way to Christ, yet all achieving the same reward. Amongst the body of saints, we will find the well-known and the unknown. St. Abraham (feast day, December 20th), a patriarchal saint, heeded God's call during the infancy of man, and brought to fruition the promise of God that his descendants would be as numerous as the stars in heaven. We also have the little known saint, St. Fidelis of Sigmaringen (April 24th), who met his death in 1622 amongst a band of Calvinists who demanded a recantation of his belief only to hear "the Catholic religion is the Faith of all ages; I fear not death." [285] We know of both the powerful and the powerless. St. Constantine (May 21st) was an emperor of Rome who issued the Edict of Milan in 313, bringing an end to the persecution of Christians. In St. Dominic (March 9th), we find a boy of only 15 years of age who instructed his fellow teenagers that "we make sanctity consist in being joyful all the time and faithfully performing our duties." [286] Amongst the Church's saints, we will find healers and we will find doctors. The Apostle St. Luke (October 18th) was a physician and a direct follower of Christ, accredited with the Gospel in his name and the Acts of the Apostles. St. Ambrose (December 7th) is one of the original four of the now thirty-three Doctors of the Church, so titled due to a three-fold condition: eminent learning, a high degree of sanctity and a proclamation by the Church. St. Ambrose, well learned and well spoken, yielded his influence in the execution of the Theodosian decrees, issued in 391 and which outlawed Pagan practices.

This Communion of Saints is wide and it is deep, all partners in Christ. You can find the sophisticated and you can find the simple. [287] St. Gregory the Great (September 3rd) was both Pope and Doctor and is known for his great contributions to the liturgy of the Mass and the Office. On the other hand, we learn herein from the simplicity of St. Thérèse (October 1st). This thirty-third Doctor of the church was so recognized not for her intellect, but rather for her "little ways", which brought child-like simplicity to the deep truths of Christ. We know of those who taught by their word and those who taught by their writings. St. John Bosco (January 31st) was known for the caring and education he brought to young boys and girls while St. Thomas Aquinas (January 28th), a Church Doctor, is known for his voluminous writings and the summary of his learnings, *Summa Theologica*. Similarly, we are blessed with those saints who have been directly healed by Christ and those

---

[285] *Lives of the Saints.*

[286] *Lives of the Saints.*

[287] *Lives of the Saints.*

who bear his pains. St. Mary Magdalene (July 22nd) was healed of her adulterous sins and comforted Christ at the foot of His cross while St. Padre Pio (September 23rd) carried the pains of Christ in the wounds of the stigmata and is considered a miracle-worker by modern day standards.

From this faithful throng, we can find traits in holiness that can serve to inspire and guide us in action. With this vast contingent of holy souls, we can find those for whom we can seek to model our lives and our behavior. We can learn from the sanctifying road traveled by this body of purity, all who walked the narrow road to Christ. However, the merits of the Communion of Saints are not limited solely to examples in holiness. These saints can also offer an exchange of holiness for our benefit and the benefit of others. "A perennial link of charity exists between the faithful who have already reached their heavenly home, those who are expiating their sins in purgatory and those who are still pilgrims on earth." [288] The work of the Communion of Saints had only just begun on earth as both salvation for their own souls and examples for the sinful or those in need. "In the treasury, too, are the prayers and good works of all the saints, all those who have followed in the footsteps of Christ the Lord and by his grace have made their lives holy and carried out the mission the Father entrusted to them. In this way they attained their own salvation and at the same time cooperated in saving their brothers in unity of the Mystical Body." [289]

The Communion of Saints is there for us. The Church highlights the saints by feast days throughout the year, giving us the opportunity to read about and learn about a different saint each and every day of the year. We also have patron saints that may bear our name-sake, to them we can develop a special and unique affiliation. We can find saints for whom we have a bond of similarity. We can seek out the saints in prayer, asking for their intercession and their support on our behalf. This holy contingent is there for us to bring profit to our desires to grow in sanctity and to gain strength in the face of sin. As Pope Paul VI wrote, "the merciful love of God and his saints is always [attentive] to our prayers." [290]

Christ's Church is thus a holy institution, founded by our Lord and guided by the

---

[288] *CCC* 1475, pg. 371 as *Indulgentiarum Doctrina*.

[289] *CCC* 1477, pg. 371 as *Indulgentiarum Doctrina*.

[290] *CCC* 962, pg. 250 as Paul VI, *Solemn Profession of Faith:* Credo of the People of God, §30.

Holy Spirit. In Christ's institution, he has provided for gifts, doctrines, teachings, sacraments, living examples, etc., all for the benefit of our spiritual edification and in support of our desire for holiness and eternal salvation. The treasury of Christ's Church knows no limits. We need to tap into this bounty. We need to expend efforts to understand and come to know the treasury that awaits our invitation. We need to avail ourselves of the gifts at our disposal. We need to act for our salvation. This is not a hidden treasure only to be discovered by a select few. Rather, it is a treasury that is readily available to all.

As you navigate the narrow road to Christ, seek the help of His institution. His Church is there for you, it is there for all, to offer light in times of darkness. Although administered by the frailty of the human essence, it remains unblemished at its core for He is the heart and soul of the Church. With St. Peter as the cornerstone of His Church, Christ built the foundation on the shoulders of His Apostles, the chosen few whom He taught and guided. By the lives they led, the oral traditions they proclaimed and the writings they left, the Apostles nurtured the infancy of His Church. We can rely on this foundation in times of question or concern. We can seek out the writings of the early Church Fathers to understand the practices they fostered. We can use our deed beads to count the occasions we seek to understand and learn from those closest to our Lord.

The early Church, under the guidance of the Holy Spirit, established the books of the Bible. We trust in His Word, the truth revealed by the Heavenly Father for his wayward sheep. Only through patience, persistence and perseverance can we come to understand and know His Word. Incarnate in His Son, the Bible is the tangible roadmap to Christ's heavenly reward. His Church not only organized His word in the books of the Bible, it also provides interpretation for the flock. The Catholic Church offers Tradition and the guidance of the Magisterium as a means to understand the life Christ has called us to. The Tradition can be found in many places at your easy disposal. It is there in footnotes and biblical commentary as well as in articles of teaching in the *Catechism*. Come to know the Bible, as well as the teaching and Tradition of His Church for "the Church's first purpose is to be a sacrament of the inner union of men with God." [291] As you seek to foster this unity with the Almighty and to grow in sanctity, use your deed beads to denote

---

[291] *CCC* 775

the time you dedicate to the reading of His Word or to understanding its meaning. Our deed beads can become a tool through which we count the ways in which we seek out and secure the truth that Christ left for us. That truth, founded in His Church, is available in countless ways. "The one mediator, Christ, established and ever sustains here on earth his holy Church, the community of faith, hope, and charity, as a visible organization through which he communicates truth and grace to all men." [292]   Count the occasions you seek to come to know that truth and to secure that grace.

One of the greatest treasures of Christ's Church is the sacrifice of the Mass which is available to us each and every day. Certainly, we need to avail ourselves of this heavenly grace each and every weekend, but we also can heighten the grace gifted us through attendance of the Mass and participation in the sacrament of the Eucharist on a more regular basis. The Mass is a hallmark of His Church, allowing us to hear His Word and to share in community fellowship as we relive His sacrifice in the transubstantiation of the bread and wine into His Body and Blood. On a daily basis, there are approximately 350,000 Catholic Masses said around the world, in almost every language and for almost every nationality. When you participate in the Mass, move more than one of your deed beads for you share in His word, you receive His sacrament of the Eucharist and you share in a treasure of His Church, the Mass. This indeed is a great step towards holiness, and all the more so when you seek out this treasure on a regular, if not, daily basis.

There are other ways to seek the treasury of His Church with consistency and regularity. In this day and time of electronic media, we can tap into faithful initiatives that can serve to prompt a daily attentiveness to the gifts of His Church. A very convenient means to find His treasury on a daily basis is to subscribe to a website that offers daily gifts from His Church. For example, a free subscription to Faith@ ND.edu offers a daily email message that contains multiple gifts from amongst His treasury. The message provides the daily reading of the Gospel, His word, as well as a beautiful commentary on an interpretation of that Word. It also offers a brief prayer in reflection to the gospel reading for the day. Lastly, it provides a synopsis of the life and characteristics of the patron saint recognized by the Church for that day. This brief and holy interlude allows for a 3-5 minute departure from the

---

[292] *CCC* 771, pg. 203 as *Lumen Gentium*.

turmoil of the day, to allow you to spend time with Him and avail yourself of gifts from the treasury of His Church. Each encounter allows you to move multiple beads on your strand as you seek to count the ways to grow in holiness.

The treasure trove that is Christ's Church is a means through which He left us all a very part of himself, ever-present to us all and in so many diverse and accessible ways. From His Word to His Body and Blood, from His teachings to His teachers, Christ established His Church that we might more easily understand and live His way. Through His Church, Christ brings constancy and purpose. The documents of Vatican II (on Dogmatic Constitutions) *Lumen Gentium* and *Sacrosanctum Concilium* provide a beautiful analogy of the birth of Christ's Church being brought forth to life through the very pangs of Christ's death on the cross. "For it was from the side of Christ as he slept the sleep of death upon the cross that there came forth the wondrous sacrament of the whole Church." [293]   St. Ambrose went on to describe that just as Eve was brought forth to life from the rib of Adam, so too was Christ's bride, His Church, brought forth to life through the piercing of Christ's heart in His sacrifice on the cross. [294] As we learn to share in His sacrifice, also learn to share in the gifts and graces that His Church has to offer. Use your deed beads to count the times and ways which you access the treasure trove of His Church. As your relationship with Christ's Church grows and blossoms, so too will your holiness grow and blossom.

---

[293] *Sacrosanctum Concilium*, 5.

[294] *CCC* 766, pg. 201 as St Ambrose, *In Luc.* 2, 85-89: J.P. Migne, ed., Patrologia Latina 15 (Paris: 1666-1668).

Contemplate:

1. What are the most important Treasures of the Church for me in my life?

2. Am I utilizing the Church's Treasury in a manner that allows me to grow closer to Jesus?

3. Will I commit to a more regular reading of the Bible?

4. How might I grow in holiness if I tap into the gifts of Christ's Holy Church?

How good Christ was to leave the

sacraments to his Church! They are

a remedy for all our needs. Venerate them

and be very grateful, both to our Lord

and to his Church.[295]

You want to be strong? Then first realize

that you are very weak. After that, trust in

Christ, your Father, your Brother,

your Teacher. He makes us strong,

entrusting to us the means with which to

conquer—the sacraments. Live them![296]

BEAD NINE

Embrace the Sacraments

Although physically Christ left His disciples when He ascended some 2000 years ago, He remained with His disciples in Spirit beginning with the descent of the Holy Spirit on Pentecost. God recognized the fallibility of fallen man and thus, centuries earlier, He made a covenant with man that He would rest His spirit on man forever and for all time. "This is my covenant with them," says the Lord. "My Spirit, which is upon you, and my words that I have put into your mouth shall never leave your mouth...from now on and forever." [297] Having received Christ's Spirit, the disciples, initially through Peter, revealed this gift to all the faithful. Following Pentecost, the first homily was delivered to the people by Peter and he readily proclaimed that they should repent and be baptized in the name of Jesus Christ the Messiah "and you will receive the gift of the Holy Spirit." [298] Thus, Christ's presence in our lives is available to all and endures forever.

Christ's life was a compilation of mysteries that are the basis of our Catholic faith today, yet His mysteries continue to draw introspection and holy interpretation by the Church's Magisterium to this very day. However, amongst the many mysteries of His life, and the gift that He was for all the world, are portals of power and grace that stand above all else for the purpose of heightening our openness to eternal salvation. These mysteries of His being are the foundations of gifts that He has offered to each of us and which are manifested in the sacraments. The sacraments are "'powers that come forth' from the Body of Christ", they are ever-living and life-giving actions of the Holy Spirit at work in His Church; they are "the masterworks of God." [299]

Amongst the treasures of His Church, Christ left sacraments for the faithful as a

---

[295] St. JoseMaria Escriva. *The Way, Furrow, the Forge*, (Scepter Publishing, New York, New York) 1988, the Way verse 521, pg. 127.

[296] St. JoseMaria Escriva. *The Way, Furrow, the Forge*, (Scepter Publishing, New York, New York) 1988, the Forge verse 643, pg. 733.

[297] Isaiah 59:21

[298] Acts 2:38

[299] *CCC* 1116

means to enable His grace to come forth and permeate through us as we routinely seek to re-align ourselves to the will of Christ. The Church recognizes that the sacraments were instituted by Jesus Christ for the salvation of souls. [300] As we seek Christ in our daily actions, we struggle with the opposing pull of the will of the world and the wayward will of fallen man. It is this threat of relativism that corrupts our path to holiness and stunts our growth in sanctity. In our weakness, we fall prey to the fallibility of man's sinfulness. In His death and resurrection, Christ overcame this imperfection of man, and He renews our ability to reorient ourselves to God through the administration of the sacraments. As St. Thomas Aquinas said, "the riches of Christ are communicated to all the members, through the sacraments." [301]

Through the sacraments, Christ confers His graces. This is the very purpose of the sacraments, "to sanctify men, to build up the Body of Christ, and, finally, to give worship to God." [302] Through the sacraments, it is neither the priest nor the recipient who is at work, but rather Christ administering His grace directly and personally. The Church affirms that sacraments provide a cloak of divine grace *ex opere operato* (literally: "by the very fact of the action's being performed"). As Saint Thomas Aquinas revealed in his masterful work of theological art, *Summa Theologica*, "the sacrament is not wrought by the righteousness of either the celebrant or the recipient, but by the power of God". [303] Even modern day theologian and Catholic convert Dr. Scott Hahn affirms the effect of this mystery as he describes sacraments as symbols, but symbols that actually and "genuinely" confer the reality they signify. Sacraments actually bring about what they signify, because it is Christ who is at work. [304]

The sacraments are a divine portal of power by which heavenly graces are bestowed on the faithful recipient. They help strengthen faith and renew the recipient's spirit of commitment to Christ. As the enlightened doctor of the Church, Saint Thomas Aquinas, further explained, "a sacrament is a sign that commemorates

---

[300] *CCC* 1114, pg. 289 as Council of Trent (1547): Denzinger-Schonmetzer, *Enchiridion Symbolorum, definitionum et declarationum de rebus fidei et morum* (1965), 1600-1601.

[301] *CCC* 947, pg. 247 as St. Thomas Acquinas, *Symb,.* 10.

[302] *CCC* 1123, pg. 291 as *Sacrosanctum Concilium* 59.

[303] *CCC* 1128, pg. 292 as St. Thomas Acquinas *Summa Theologica* III,68, 8.

[304] Scott Hahn. *Swear to God, The Promise and Power of the Sacraments* (Random House, Inc, New York, New York), 2003, pg.18.

what precedes it – Christ's Passion; demonstrates what is accomplished in us through Christ's Passion – grace; and prefigures what the Passion pledges to us – future glory." [305] Sacraments bring nourishment to our faith and sustain us on the narrow road to Christ. Recall the call of our Master, "be perfect, just as your heavenly Father is perfect." [306] This is an unattainable state for us individually; however, by the gift and graces of our Father, in alignment with His will, we can reach sanctity and eternal salvation in heaven. On that journey, His sacraments can offer us a moment in perfection, in unity with His grace, and can elevate our state of holiness.

There are seven sacraments in the Church that each confer grace in different ways and bring sustenance to us in different stages and aspects of our faith-filled journey in Christ. These seven sacraments can be viewed in various ways, a common way however is to separate them into the sacraments of initiation (3), the sacraments of healing (2), and the two sacraments of service, that build up the Body of Christ.

For most Christians, Christ's open invitation to eternal salvation begins through the sacrament of Baptism. One of the three sacraments of initiation, Baptism opens the gates to His gift for eternal life. In Baptism, we are born anew, and Christ confers on the recipient freedom from sin and death. Liberated from the shackles of damnation, Baptism is a sharing in God's divine nature and represents the invitation and incorporation into Christ's Church. "Baptism is a bath of water in which the 'imperishable seed' of the Word of God produces its life-giving effect." [307]

Baptism is celebrated by a cleansing of water, just as John the Baptist did to penitents in the river Jordan. In accord with the practice of the celebration, the efficacious effect of the rite brings freedom from Original Sin. Any transient separation from God from Original Sin or personal sin, is relinquished in this life-giving sacrament. So too is punishment for this sin. As proclaimed at the Council of Florence in 1439, "in those who have been reborn nothing remains that would impede their entry into the Kingdom of God, neither Adam's sin, nor personal sin, nor the consequences of sin, the gravest of which is separation from God." [308]

---

[305] *CCC* 1130, pg. 292 as St. Thomas Acquinas *Summa Theologica* III,60, 3.

[306] Matthew 5:48

[307] *CCC* 1228

[308] *CCC* 1263

Not only does Baptism provide purification from sin, but it also avails the recipient of a rebirth in the Holy Spirit. A new creature emerges from the holy water, an adopted son and daughter of the Almighty, who has received an invitation to partake of His Divine Nature. [309] From the portal of power for the Baptized comes the gift of sanctifying grace, notably the grace of justification. The Baptized is now fortified with the grace of faith and hope in the Heavenly King, with the power to feel and act under the promptings of the Holy Spirit and with the grace to grow in moral virtue. [310] For the baptized, the divine seed has now been planted.

Baptism also confers the grace of unity with Christ's Church. The baptized are all members of His Body and His Church. "As a body is one though it has many parts, and all the parts of the body, though many, are one body, so also Christ. For in one Spirit we were all baptized into one body." [311] Through baptism, a sacramental bond of unity now exists, calling all baptized into the fraternity of God's children, those who call themselves Christians of this world. A parting gift from this sacramental union with God's family is the indelible seal of eternal life, the spiritual mark for the day of redemption known as the *Dominicus character.* [312] The Baptized are now marked with the symbol of the Almighty for He has "put his seal upon us and given the Spirit in our hearts as a first installment." [313] Baptism cannot be repeated.

The salvific sacrament of Holy Communion, partaking in the divine banquet of Christ, is not only a sacrament of initiation, but it is the gift of eternal life with Christ. We know that Christ's ways are not our ways, yet it is His ways that lead to everlasting life. His words were plain and clear, yet hard for many to accept: "I am the living bread that came down from heaven; whoever eats this bread will live forever; and the bread that I give is my flesh for the life of the world." [314] Many in the crowd in Capernaum that day heard His words, but had eyes not to see nor ears to understand. They saw him only as the son of the carpenter Joseph and his wife Mary, and not as one sent from heaven above. They failed to see in

---

[309] *CCC* 1265

[310] *CCC* 1266

[311] 1 Corinthians 12:13-14

[312] *CCC* 1274

[313] 2 Corinthians 1:22

[314] John 6:51

Christ that he was the true bread of life in the same way that God had, centuries before, rained down manna to sustain their ancestors with food in the desert. From their lack of trust and understanding the crowd again asked Jesus for a sign, even though their bellies were still full from the miraculous multiplication of loaves just hours before. Although often our Lord spoke in parables as He sought to teach the crowd, here He speaks in plain truth and reaffirms the banquet that He offers via Himself for all who choose to believe. He does not relent in the simple truth that he revealed, but He persists in this truth to the disbelief of many in Capernaum and for many even today: "Amen, amen, I say to you, unless you eat the flesh of the Son of Man and drink his blood, you do not have life within you. Whoever eats my flesh and drinks my blood has eternal life, and I will raise him on the last day. For my flesh is true food, and my blood is true drink. Whoever eats my flesh and drinks my blood remains in me and I in him." [315] Regrettably, many of His disciples did not remain in Him because they could not believe His truth and these left and returned to their former way of life. To these, Christ did not recant His proclamation. No, Christ remained firm to His Holy truth. Fortunately for us, Christ has left us a seat at His banquet in the sustaining sacrament of Holy Communion.

Miraculously, what is contained within the unleavened bread of Holy Communion is the "sum and summary of our faith". [316] Through this enduring and replenishing sacrament of initiation, comes the divine life of Christ for us individually and for the communion of the faithful. He comes in a most welcoming and sustaining fashion and draws us deeper into the depths of His grace with each partaking of His life-giving offering. From this beautiful sacrament, we acquire more willful alignment with God's will and with His way. We are strengthened in charity and gain strength in the face of sin and temptation. His life is heightened in us and we are united with the body faithful. Our communion with His Church is active and alive.

The Eucharist is raised above all other sacraments and it is indeed the pinnacle of our faith and all other sacraments "are oriented to it." [317] Doctor of the Church, St. Thomas Aquinas, taught of the riches of the sacrament of Holy Communion

---

[315] John 6:53-56

[316] *CCC* 1327

[317] *CCC* 1324, pg. 334 as *Presbyterorum Ordinis* 5.

when he wrote that the Eucharist is "the perfection of the spiritual life and the end to which all the sacraments tend." [318] Yet, the riches of this beautiful gift are founded in faith and faith alone. It cannot be reasoned and has been the cause of not only a desertion in the ranks of disciples in Christ's earthly day, but also in the separation of countless Christian faithful. Many have come to appreciate that His true Body and Blood cannot be reasoned by the senses, but only by faith in His word. For as St. Cyril proclaimed, "do not doubt whether this is true, but rather receive the words of the Savior in faith, for since He is the truth, he cannot lie." [319]

Confirmation fulfills the third sacrament of initiation within Christ's Church as well as brings to full fruition the gift of grace received in Baptism. In Confirmation, the recipient is fortified with the gifts of the Holy Spirit. For the recipient, reception into the Body of Christ's Church, which is brought forth initially in Baptism, now becomes fully realized and strengthened. Perfumed oil, or chrism, is used to anoint the recipient with the laying on of hands by the bishop, and the imprinting of a spiritual seal. This seal perfects our entrance into Christ's family and guarantees the divine protection of our Heavenly Father. For Jesus taught His Disciples that He would not leave them orphans, but rather, His Father would leave them another Advocate: "I have told you this while I am with you. The Advocate, the Holy Spirit, that the Father will send in my name-He will teach you everything and remind you of all that I told you." [320]

Confirmation completes Baptism by deepening the gift of spiritual grace and more firmly uniting us to Christ. The gifts of the Holy Spirit are now fully available to the Confirmed. The initiation is fulfilled and we will carry His seal for eternity. The voice of Christ and the inclinations of truth, love, and wisdom, are now part of the inherent make-up of our soul. The sacrament of Confirmation completes and fulfills Christ's grace of initiation into His Body and into His Church.

Just as any parent seeks to bring comfort and healing to his or her ailing child, so too does the Almighty seek to offer consolation and healing to us. The two sacraments of healing, Reconciliation and Anointing of the Sick, are indeed two miraculous sacraments that bring the Divine Hands of our Maker to a holy embrace of our stricken souls. The sacrament of Reconciliation is known by other names as well, Penance and Confession, however regardless of the name the effects of the sacrament are life-giving and life-saving.

We receive unity with Christ and His Church when perfected by the three sacraments of initiation, however, our sinfulness creates a drift from Christ's Way and leads to actions that are juxtaposed to His call to us to be and remain holy. It is an uphill climb to holiness and we often stumble along the way. The climb however is the journey we all are on, and we need respite and reprieve from the many times we find ourselves disoriented and distracted from the path Christ has laid before us. Remember, however, it is His Way and we are invited to follow. He fully understands and appreciates the difficulties we encounter, and for this reason the fount of his mercy endures forever and is endless in its magnitude.

The sacrament of Reconciliation is truly the long sought after fountain of youth for it is where countless souls can come to receive eternal rejuvenation and life-restoring mercy. How can we walk by such a gift-giving sacrament and not seek to partake of the grace of God's mercy? It is only our pride that can keep us from enjoying the eternal fruits of reunification with our Divine Maker. Fear not. Open your heart to the gift that awaits you in the confessional. Whether you last went to Confession 20 years ago or two, it matters not, the gift is there for no one other than for you specifically. It is your decision; can you rise above any fear of minor embarrassment in verbalizing your sins before God's priestly proxy? You can and you must for this sacrament brings divine healing to our souls, healing we can find in the hands of no other. Due to our inherent inclination towards sin, our concupiscence, we need Christ's merciful lifeline.

Recall the most well-known of Christ's parables, that of the Prodigal Son. The Father's loving embrace awaited his wayward son who took advantage of the love and gifts of his Father, only to return humbled by his indiscretion and sinfulness. But the story only begins there as the Father lovingly draws his son back in and restores him to full unity for "he was dead and has come to life again; he was lost and has been found." [321] Think also of the gift of Paradise that the Good Thief received as a result of his confession to Christ on the cross. He knew of and admitted to his sinfulness and for this, he received Christ's merciful absolution,

---

[318] St. Thomas Acquinas *Summa Theologica* III,73, 3c.

[319] *CCC* 1381, pg. 348 as St. Thomas Acquinas *Summa Theologica* III,75, 1.

[320] John 14:25-26

[321] Luke 15:32

"Amen, I say to you, today you will be with me in Paradise." [322]

Seek out the Father's divine mercy in the confessional and enjoy the resulting freedom and purity that follows. Just as all enjoy that new car clean and smell, so too do we enjoy the return to that state of cleanliness and newness after a deep clean and detailing that restores the car to its original state. Allow the confessional to become the carwash to our souls, bringing a deep, new clean and shiny hue to the blessed soul Christ has planted within us. Tear asunder your pride and run to the calming and merciful graces found in the confessional.

Healing also is available in times of need through the sacrament of Anointing of the Sick. This special sacrament is for those who may be terminally ill and in need of God's healing grace at the hour of a pending death for which it may be referred to as "Extreme Unction". Alternatively, the sacrament can also be reserved for one in need of the Father's special grace whether it be due to frailty of old age, a pending procedure that carries risk to one's life, or an advancing illness. This sacrament can be received more than once and is administered only by a priest who lays his hands upon the infirmed and prays over them with the faith of the Church. Holy oil, blessed by the bishop, is used to anoint the forehead. The Eucharist can follow for those at the hour of imminent death as the last sacrament along the earthly journey, known as "viaticum" for passing into Christ's hands and the journey home.

The sacrament of Anointing of the Sick confers several graces which bring healing to the infirmed. It connects the recipient spiritually to the Passion of Christ and brings strength and courage to endure the illness. It can confer physical health if it be the will of the Father, but always confers spiritual healing. It also draws in the gift of God's eternal mercy for all committed sin. It is the antidote to our spiritual infirmity from the master physician, our Lord Jesus Christ.

Lastly, we turn to the two sacraments of service, which bring strength and unity to Christ's Church. The sacraments of Holy Orders and Matrimony bring salvation to others and are founded upon a grace received from the Father for the benefit of others.

---

[322] Luke 23:43

In the sacrament of Holy Orders, Christ confers His sacred power on His anointed ministers on earth who are tasked with shepherding His flock. These ministers are called to carry on His apostolic mission by acting "in persona Christi Capitis" [323] through which the ordained is now called and consecrated to "act in the power and place of the person of Christ himself." [324] This does not mean that the minister is devoid of all human weakness and sin as we saw first-hand in the failings of the great apostle Peter, but rather that the ordained is called to serve the Almighty and to facilitate the fruits of His grace through the administration of His sacraments and the celebration of the Mass. Through the sacrament of Holy Orders, Christ continues to lead his Church and to bring grace to those who seek Him.

Among the original twelve tribes of Israel, it was the Levites who inherited God's call to ministerial and liturgical service. The Levite priests were "taken from among men and made their representatives before God, to offer gifts and sacrifices for sins." [325] Today, in the sacrament of Holy Orders, the bishop lays his hands on the ordained with consecratory prayer to affirm the gift of the Holy Spirit now representing Christ before the faithful assembly of His Church. As confirmed by the Council of Trent (1545-1564), the sacrament of Holy Orders "confers an indelible spiritual character and cannot be repeated or conferred temporarily." [326]

The second of the sacraments of service is the sacrament of Matrimony whereby God the Father imparts an indelible and unbreakable spiritual bond of unity between a man and a woman, between a husband and a wife. It is here that an authentic human love is drawn in and co-mixed with a divine love. [327] The blessing received in the sacrament of Matrimony is a special grace that enables one spouse to help the other to grow in holiness. [328] The spiritual growth of the spouses also facilitates the fundamental task of creating new life for God's world and nurturing that life towards holiness.

---

[323] *CCC* 548, pg. 387 as *Lumen Gentium* 10; 28.

[324] *CCC* 1548, pg. 387 as Pope Pius XII, *Mediator Dei:* AAS, 39 (1947), 548.

[325] Hebrews 5:1

[326] *CCC* 1582, pg. 395 as Council of Trent: Denzinger-Schonmetzer, *Enchiridion Symbolorum, definitionum et declarationum de rebus fidei et morum* (1965), 1767.

[327] *CCC* 1639, pg. 409 as *Gaudium et Spes* 48 § 2.

[328] *CCC* 1641, pg. 409 as *Lumen Gentium* 11 § 2.

In the sacrament of Matrimony, the priest, as a witness for and a representative of the Church, receives the consent of the man and the woman and provides a blessing on behalf of the Church. Christ now co-exists in the bond of unity between a husband and a wife and it is He who facilitates and sanctifies them on the way to eternal life. [329]

The seven sacraments are each unique in the gift of grace that Christ imparts to the faithful recipient. Avail yourself of the sacraments of the Church, instituted by Christ that we might grow in holiness.

Imagine we are a sailboat drifting at sea, struggling with the constant ebb and flow of the untiring ocean currents. Our struggle persists without direction and with an unending battle of exertion against the power of the sea. A struggle we will lose if left to drift on our own accord. However, our vessel is equipped with the potential for directional relief found in the stability of the mast and the expanse of the sail. With the sail set, we gain direction and power. We can right our vessel and seek the direction we need to bring us home. Our sail represents the life-giving grace and direction we receive anew each time in the portals of power found in the sacraments. Our sail, the sacraments, reorients our way and propels us in our intended direction. Yet, our sail requires the foundation of the mast (which represents the Church) to ensure it is properly oriented and grounded, and the willful effort on our part in making the sail effective in finding its course. Without our attention to the sail and our commitment to make the sail effective, the sail brings no value to the excursion and we will drift aimlessly. Conversely, if we use the sail to our advantage, and rely on the effect the sail can bring to the vessel, we can reorient our way and propel ourselves forward. Through it all, our Heavenly Father is the wind that has no rest and is hidden, but always present in our day. He brings life and power to the sail and allows us to soar to our destination.

On our journey towards sanctity we need to seek out the blessed graces found in Christ's life-giving and life-restoring sacraments. Our efforts towards holiness can be enhanced if we continually seek to access the sacraments that are available to us and in appreciating the sacraments that have a daily impact on our lives and on those for whom we cherish. Practice using your deed beads each and every day

---

[329] *CCC* 1661, pg. 414 as *Gaudium et Spes* 48 § 2.

to count the ways that the sacraments have an effect on your life or alternatively on the lives of others. Learn to become attentive to the divine intervention Christ offers in each day through the effects of the sacraments, through His portals of divine grace. The gifts of the sacraments can be obvious or they can be subtle, yet our ascent in holiness can be enhanced when we fully embrace the sacraments both in receiving them and in appreciating and being attentive to the daily gifts they impart.

We embrace the sacraments fully when we receive them directly. However, we also reap benefits from the graces transferred in the sacraments when we learn to recognize the ongoing subtleties of the graces conferred. For instance, consider the following examples for which we can count the ways using our deed beads of God's divine gifts that emanate from the various sacraments. In Baptism, we should take note of the beauty of family and Godparents intermingled with the sacrament of Baptism as well as the entrance of a new member to the confraternity of Christians. At mass, take delight in knowing that the infants you see at mass and in the cry rooms have been blessed by parents who seek their eternal well-being and for the baptismal removal of any remnant of Original Sin and the invitation to Christ's eternal salvation.

For Holy Eucharist, we should certainly take note of the times we receive the Body and Blood of Christ. However, with our deed beads, we should also take note of the times we enjoy the company of Christ in Adoration, or when we see a fellow parishioner taking the Eucharist in a pyx (Eucharist holder) to an infirmed friend seeking to receive His Body, or when we think of or speak of the true presence of Christ in the species of consecrated unleavened bread and consecrated wine. We should embrace the gift of this life-giving sacrament and celebrate it when we stand tall in the face of criticism from those who erroneously profess that Christ's true presence is only "symbolic". He is truly present in the miraculous gift of the Eucharist and we should affirm this in our thoughts and in our actions at all times.

In Confirmation, we should celebrate the gift of sponsorship by one member of Christ's community toward another who is seeking to receive the Holy Spirit. We should celebrate the saints who have been chosen by the Confirmandi. With the sliding of our deed bead, we can count the ways of adolescents who "choose" Christ by their actions or those who seek to celebrate the "truth" of Christ in their youth groups and parish ministries. Teenagers who challenge the worldly norms of the school hallways and who swim upstream against the pressures of peer by choosing Christ, chastity, purity and morality; these are the true stewards of Christ's Church. We need to be attentive to this faith-filled heroism and move the beads on our strand as we too grow in holiness by our recognition of the Holy Spirit at work.

From the sacrament of Reconciliation, not only should we benefit by divine cleansing from this beautiful sacrament, but we should also move our beads as we grow in holiness when we practice penance, or dedicate our day via the daily offering, or embrace a cross for the greater glory of God. We can take a step in holiness when we fast or sacrifice or speak of the depths of the Almighty's mercy. Remember, His hour is 3:00 pm each and every day, the time during which we can grow in sanctity by a thought-filled moment of prayer and thanksgiving for the suffering He endured and for the endless mercy that He offers. Reconciliation abounds and His mercy is for all. We take a step in holiness when we make this gift a part of our day and our life.

In the sacrament of Anointing of the Sick, we appreciate the gift of healing that the Father brings to those in need. However, we too can grow in holiness as we align our prayers to those needing health, or when we provide comfort and assistance to the infirmed. Our efforts towards healing for another are examples of stewardship towards the community of Christ and the gift of comfort and healing we can bring to those in need. Our prayers for the well-being of others are significant and represent holiness in action.

The sacrament of Holy Orders confers a beautiful seal of brotherhood for the ministry of Christ's Church. However, we too can grow in the grace of this sacrament through prayerful intentions for those who shepherd His Church. We can count our steps in sanctity when we pray for a growth in vocations or speak well of and defend those who lead the flock. The hurdle is high for these ministers of Christ and our prayers, support and alignment to their ministry is a testament to our holiness amongst the community of Christ's Church.

Lastly, the sacrament of matrimony brings sustenance to us all as the baton of the miracle of life is passed from generation to generation. Not only can we celebrate and share in the sacrament of matrimony directly in our own marriage, but also we can celebrate the marriages of those who have sustained and embraced a commitment towards unity of love and purpose. Wedding Anniversaries celebrate this commitment and we should recognize the gift of God at work. So too can we move our deed beads when we take notice of the divine love of the Father at work in the relationship of husband and wife, be it a simple holding of hands, a loving embrace, or a display of true and unifying love. The gift of marriage is profound, the love expressed is sanctity. We need to celebrate this love and be attentive to it in all its subtleties.

Christ left us seven unique sacraments through which we can receive His portal of power and Divine grace. Some sacraments occur on a single occasion; others we can embrace more often. The gifts of grace are directly conferred in each of the seven sacraments, but so too does Christ impart graces to those who are on the path toward sanctity when we find the face of Christ in the most subtle and sublime ways. Using our deed beads, we can increase our attentiveness to the whisper of his word and the embrace He offers in so many quiet and subtle ways. It is in learning to recognize these daily gifts and seeking to appreciate Christ's divine graces that we learn to become more attentive to the flow of Christ's divinity in our day. This is the attentiveness we need, through little ways, to grow in holiness.

Contemplate:

1. Do I understand the gift of each of Christ's seven sacraments?

2. Will I commit to receiving Christ regularly in the Sacrament of Holy Eucharist?

3. Will I commit to going to Confession?

4. How great would I feel after I make my next Confession?

"Nonne cor nostrum ardens erat in nobis, dum loqueretur in via?" "Was not our heart burning within us, while he spoke to us on the way?" If you are an apostle, these words of the disciples of Emmaus should rise spontaneously to the lips of your professional companions when they meet you along the ways of their lives [330]

BEAD TEN

Be an Ambassador for Christ

The evening was dark, the wind was howling and the waves were thrashing against the listless boat that fought the onslaught of the sea's power. The boat was being tossed and soon would be taking on water. Huddled in the boat were Christ's 12 disciples, wet, in fear and afraid of the torrents that would soon overtake them. We know what happens in St. Mark's gospel account, where next we learn that Christ, who happens to be walking along on the water, gets into the boat. "But at once he [Jesus] spoke with them, 'Take courage, it is I, do not be afraid!' He got into the boat with them and the wind died down." [331] Christ responds to the fear that He sees in His disciples by settling the wind and calming the sea. On countless occasions, we have studied and discussed the miracles that St. Mark reports, the power of Christ to walk on the water and to have command over the wind and the sea. Truly amazing yes! However, there is more here, it is a very subtle point that we often overlook, yet its implications speak eternal volumes about what God the Father has offered to us all in His only begotten Son. That is, Christ was fully Divine, He was and is all powerful. He walked on water and had full and complete dominion over nature through His power over the wind and the sea. As the alpha and the omega, the beginning and the end, He did not, and does not need us! Christ could easily have continued on His way. He did not need to concern Himself with the fear and helplessness of His disciples. He could have walked on His way and passed the boat! The amazing miracle and the gift that He offers us all, is that He didn't pass by the boat, but rather He stopped and climbed in the boat! He, the Divine, humbled Himself and got into our boat!

St. Paul summarizes this miracle beautifully in his introduction to the Ephesians when he writes, "In love, he destined us for adoption to himself through Jesus Christ, in accord with the favor of his will, for the praise of the glory of his grace that he granted us in the beloved." [332] God the Father has chosen to allow us to

---

[330] St. JoseMaria Escriva. *The Way, Furrow, the Forge,* (Scepter Publishing, New York, New York) 1988, the Way verse 917, pg. 234.

[331] Mark 6:50-51

[332] Ephesians 1:4-6

glimpse His boundless divinity and He has made us His children whom He loves and to whom He has offered eternal salvation. Most often however, just as we likely missed the splendor in Christ's selfless act of getting in our boat, do we also miss Him acting in our lives.

We have all enjoyed the occasional challenge of looking at optical illusions and trying to bring clarity to a picture intended to create confusion. For instance, in viewing the illusion below, one might readily describe the two faces that are staring at each other. To many, it is clear that two faces are in the drawing in black outlined with a white outline. However, for all those that see only the two faces, they might be surprised to hear from another that the picture is actually that of a chalice drawn in white color on a black background. Both are actually correct as is consistent with the intent of the optical illusion, however in a broader context this illusion reinforces the idea that we often do not see the "faces" or the "chalice" because we do not allow ourselves the time or opportunity to reflect upon it. We see what we want to see. Henceforth however, we may be more likely in the future to focus on the full and complete picture which not only includes the black faces, but also includes the white chalice.

[www.pinterest.com]

So too is Christ always present in our lives. Yet, all too frequently, we focus on the noise and bustle of our lives, and fail to find Christ there amongst our day. We are easily distracted by our own worldly interests and concerns. However, He is there in the middle of our every thought and our every action. We on the other hand, go about our day, focused on our immediate needs, focused on what drives us and motivates us forward all the while failing to see that Christ is there with us, step by step, little way by little way. Recall the Old Testament's story of Elijah.

As the prophet was fleeing for his life in fear of Jezebel who wanted to take his life, he sought guidance from God the Father. Where did Elijah find God? He did not find God in the strong and heavy wind, nor the earthquake, nor the fire. But rather, Elijah found the Father in a "tiny whispering sound", at which uttering Elijah hid his face in his cloak so as not to look directly upon the Lord. [333] In the New Testament, we know all too well Christ's teaching from St. Matthew's gospel, "Lord of heaven and earth, for although you have hidden these things from the wise and the learned you have revealed them to the childlike". [334] So it is in childlike humility that we will find Him. He is there, He chose us, He got into our boat... and He is expecting something of us. "It was not you who chose me, but I who chose you and appointed you to go and bear fruit!" [335]

In Christ's command that we "go and bear fruit", He is asking us to be active participants in His ministry. To be His disciples, we must engage in the lives of others as peacemakers, bringing and displaying Christ's message of love. We are called to get into the boat of other people's lives by being charitable, loving and makers of peace. After partaking in His everlasting sustenance in the Eucharist at Mass, what do Christ's shepherds commission us to do? The priest closes the Mass with the call for us each to "Go forth to love and serve the Lord". Author Jim Forest highlights this special call to action when he writes, "having been privileged to take part in the Eucharist, we are returned to the world as ambassadors of Christ's peace." [336] We have been called by Our Lord to action!

We have been introduced to one of the greatest servers of our Lord, St. Francis of Assisi. He believed and practiced the art of active engagement into the lives of others. St. Francis is known to have said "Preach the Gospel at all times, if necessary, use words." [337] With his well-documented actions of benevolence, his simple and austere livelihood, clothed in a rough, brown garment, and persistence in his proclamations of Christ's teachings to all, Francis grew in acclaim. Soon brother compatriots joined his way as friars that soon came to be known appropriately

---

[333] 1 Kings 19:12

[334] Matthew 11:25

[335] John 15:16

[336] Jim Forest, *The Ladder of the Beatitudes*, (Orbis Books, Maryknoll, New York) 1999, pg 111.

[337] http://www.capuchinfranciscans.org/blog/preach-the-gospel-at-all-times-if-necessary-use-words

as Franciscans. Francis required one rule, the Primitive Rule, which was "To follow the teachings and footprints of our Lord Jesus Christ." [338]   St. Francis chose to get into the boat of other's lives and to not sit idle. He chose to walk in the footsteps of Christ and to actively engage with others. He was a maker of peace.

Author Jim Forest highlights this very fact in his writings on the call to action found in the Beatitudes. The seventh Beatitude was not a call to be wishers for peace, awaiters of peace or searchers for peace. In Christ's Sermon on the Mount, He calls us each to be "makers" of peace, and to these peacemakers, they will be Blessed and they shall be called children of God. This was Christ's call to action. He actively chose to get into our boat and in choosing us, He has called us to actively get into the boat of others. He has called us to action, to bear fruit, to be makers of peace. Who is called to be makers of peace? "It is each of us. The beatitude of peacemaking is part of ordinary Christian life in all its daily-ness." [339] In so doing, we all become children of God. As His children, we now fulfill the beautiful words of St. Paul's letter to the Ephesians where God willed our adoptions to himself through Jesus Christ. [340]

In his book *The Ladder of the Beatitudes*, Jim Forest goes on to further expound upon our relationship to others and our duty to love them. Forest explains the image of the wheel described by the desert Saint Dorotheos of Gaza as descriptive of our comingled relationship between love of God and love of neighbor. In the wheel, God is the center-point. Mankind is the periphery represented by the circumference of the wheel. This circle is our world and the life of each of God's beings journeys along a line from the perimeter to the center-point (God). "The straight line drawn from the circumference to the center are the lives of men," writes Forest. [341] By the very act of progressing along our individual line towards holiness and unity with God, we also grow closer in unity to our neighbor. Forest describes that "if we were to love God more, we should be closer to God, and through love of him we should be more united in love to our neighbor; and the more we are united to our neighbor the more we are united to God." [342] Thus our love is not singular, we don't practice love that exists solely between God and

---

[338] A RECONSTRUCTION OF THE 'PRIMITIVE' RULE OF SAINT FRANCIS (1209/1210) from the Regula non Bullata (1221), www. tssf.org.uk/wp-content/uploads/.../1_The_Primitive_Rule_of_St_Francis_1209.pdf.

[339] Jim Forest, pg. 126.

[340] Ephesians 1:4-6.

[341] Jim Forest, pg 129.

self. Rather, our love of God impacts those around us, those we interact with, and their love of God impacts us. Our lives and love our interrelated and co-mingled.

Challenged by Christ's call to action, to be ambassadors for Christ, we might wonder where and how to begin. As with everything in Christ, prayer is a great place to start. Just as the picture of the two faces also always contains the chalice, so too for us, Christ is there always, but we need to pay closer attention to His presence and learn to more readily hear Him amongst the noise of our day. He is always there in our lives and He is bringing calm and direction to our boat. Reach out to Him in prayer that He will illuminate your path forward.

Remember the prayer of the blind man, Bartimaeus, in Chapter 10 of St. Mark's Gospel. While begging along the roadside to Jericho, Bartimaeus calls out in desperation to Jesus who happens to be passing by with a sizable crowd. Hearing his call, Jesus brings Bartimaeus forward. What is it you are seeking of Me, Jesus inquires. Bartimaeus replies, "Master, I want to see." Jesus responds that his faith has saved him and immediately Bartimaeus received his sight. Christ awaits us too. We too can pray for a clearer vision as to how we can walk and live more faithfully

Do you know Jabez, a distant descendant of King David? Bruce Wilkinson writes eloquently about Jabez throughout his whole book entitled, The Prayer of Jabez. [344] However, it is only in 1 Chronicles Chapter 4, verse 9 and 10 that we learn all that we know about Jabez. How can so much be written about someone for whom we know so little? The answer is found in the magnitude of God's response to Jabez's simple yet profound prayer. Jabez seeks God in prayer and asks God "Oh, that you may truly bless me and extend my boundaries! Help me and make me free of misfortune, without pain!" "And, God grants his prayer." [345] Jabez asks God for His blessing and he asks God to expand his boundaries. Jabez is asking God to walk with him as he moves into new territories, territories that God is calling him to enter. Jabez asks for God's help that He might lead him. God grants Jabez his prayer! Faithfully we too should call to God to bless us and expand our territories. We too should call out to God to help us! Calling Christ into our boat

[342] Jim Forest, pg 129.

[343] Mark 10:51

[344] Bruce Wilkinson. The Prayer of Jabez: Breaking Through to the Blessed Life, (Multnomah Publishers, Inc., Sisters Oregon) 2000.

[345] 1 Chronicles 4:10

will strengthen us as we seek to step into the boats of other's lives. In faith and in prayer we can become ambassadors for Christ. In calling to the Father in prayer, He will hear us and He will answer us, just as He did for Jabez.

On our journey towards sanctity, seek ways to become holy to others. As we have seen in St. Thérèse, in Saint Francis, and in Saint Teresa of Calcutta, the hand we extend into the lives of others does not need to be grandiose. Even the subtlest efforts can make an impact. This very thought was prayerfully expressed in the September 29, 2015 novena prayed on PrayMoreNovenas.com where all those participating prayed:

> "Today, let's pray for an emptying out of ourselves so that we can be Christ to others. Let's pray for the realization that our lives may be the only Gospel that some people ever read.

> With that in mind let us continue on with our daily activities and responsibilities as St. Thérèse would. Doing small things with great love for the Glory of God." [346]

It is amazing that we can actually bring the Gospel to life and to action by the efforts we extend to others. What we do in our actions and with our physical bodies can impact our inner sanctity. Pope Pius XI wrote that with our physical bodies we can "serve as instruments for the interior sanctification of our souls, or to use the words of the Apostle Paul, as instruments of justice unto God." [347] We can do God's will and grow closer to Him in holiness by being His Ambassador to others. Christ asked and challenged His closest friends, His disciples, to preach to people everywhere. In fact, Jesus' earliest lesson upon meeting His newest disciples along the Sea of Galilee, Peter and Andrew, was "Come after me, and I will make you fishers of men." [348] The last of Jesus' instructions came after His Resurrection shortly before His Ascension when He commissioned His disciples to "Go into the whole world and proclaim the gospel to every creature." [349] Seek to fulfill the role Christ commissioned to each of us. Be an instrument of peace and become an oar in the boat of your neighbor.

We can be an active instrument in the lives of others, helping propel them towards

---

[346] www.PrayMoreNovenas.com.

[347] Piux XI. Quas primas, 11 December 1925, 21

[348] Matthew 4:19

[349] Mark 16:15

Christ. We can find little ways to be an ambassador for Christ. Using our Deed Beads we can count the ways in which we act upon Christ's call for us to become active participants in His ministry. In a gospel reflection published by the University of Notre Dame, Bob Pfunder proposed relevant questions that we each should be asking ourselves: "To what and to whom am I leading those around me? Are my words and deeds leading those around me to the hope of the kingdom, to Jesus?" [350] The ways we can help lead others to Christ are numerous. We can lend an ear to a friend in need. We can assist a stranger. We can openly speak of Christ and share His greeting. We can join in a community effort by volunteering our time and talent. We can visit and pray for the infirmed. We can avoid gossip and judgment. We can express forgiveness and be merciful. We can show kindness and love to our family, friends, strangers and enemies. We can mend a broken relationship. We can give to the less fortunate and protect and shelter the vulnerable. We are not limited for we must remember that even in smallness can there be found the mighty and the grand. Christ illustrated the power of the small when he taught that "like a mustard seed that, when it is sown in the ground, is the smallest of all the seeds on the earth. But once it is sown, it springs up and becomes the largest of plants and puts forth large branches, so that the birds of the sky can dwell in its shade." [351]   G.K. Chesterson wrote that "the Saint is a medicine because he is an antidote…he is not what the people [may] want, but rather what the people need." [352]

Yes, it is very possible for us to have a profound impact on the lives of others and in so doing, on our very own salvation. In choosing to be an active participant in Christ's ministry, in choosing to step into the boat of other's lives, as Christ did for each of us, we take a step forward in sanctity. Just as Christ is an active part of our lives, He commissions us each to become a part of the lives' of others. Michael Gaitley described this call when he wrote that "preparing the world for the Lord's final coming is really about becoming saints ourselves and helping others to become saints, too." [353]   This should be a goal of ours for each and every day, that is, to seek ways to bring Christ to the lives of others. In the beautiful Christ the King

---

[350] Bob Pfunder, *www.Pray.nd.edu*, July 12, 2012

[351] Mark 4:31-32

[352] Richard Conlin, St. Thomas Aquinas by GK Chesterton, https://richardconlin.wordpress.com/2014/08/30/st-thomas-aquinas-by-gk-chesterton, August 30, 2014.

[353] Michael Gaitley, *The Second Greatest Story Ever Told*, 2015.

novena in preparation for Christ the King Feast Day, those participating prayed:

> "I beg You to show me mercy and give me the grace to become a great saint. I pray that not only will I spend eternity with You but that You may use me – a sinner – to bring others into Your Kingdom for Your glory." [354]

Let us therefore strive to be that instrument of peace, to bring joy to the lives of others. Greg Aitchison aptly described the beauty of this joy when he wrote:

> "One quote I often repeat to my students is: 'If you want joy, live with J.O.Y. (Jesus first, Others second, Yourself third).
>
> We are all called to be saints—people who let God into their lives and then give their lives away. May we all choose to live with J.O.Y. this day and the rest of our lives!" [355]

We know Saint Mother Teresa was one of the greatest examples of living Christ's call to holiness by interceding in the lives of the less fortunate. The degree of this call is different for everyone, but Christ has issued a call to each of us to be His ambassadors. Saint Teresa of Calcutta described this call to her Missionaries of Charity Sisters when she instructed them that "It is only when we realize our nothingness, our emptiness, that God can fill us with Himself. When we become full of God then we can give God to others, for from the fullness of the heart the mouth speaks." [356] She also revealed that Christ's inner spark for her came from an interior locution where she heard the voice of Jesus command, "Come, come, carry Me into the homes of the poor. Come, be My light." [357]

Let us each be the light of Christ for others and for the world and let us count our luminosity with our deed beads each time that we shine Christ's light on our neighbor.

[354] www.PrayMoreNovenas.com, November 16, 2015

[355] Greg Aitchison, www.Pray.nd.edu.

[356] Mother Theresa, *Where There is Love, There is God:* A Path to Closer Union with God and Greater Love for Others, (Crown Publishing Group), August 2010.

[357] Brian Kolodiejchuk. *Mother Teresa, Come Be My Light,* the private writings of the "Saint of Calcutta", Mother Teresa to the Mission of Charity Sisters first Friday, November 1960.

Contemplate:

1. How might the world change if more people heard Jesus' call to be an Ambassador for Him?

2. Do I believe that I can make a stronger commitment to being an Ambassador for Christ?

3. What are some of the ways that I can step into the boat of other's lives and make a contribution that is Christ-like?

4. What might your family, friend or neighbor say about you in thanksgiving?

CONCLUSION

"My son (and daughter), you are here with me always, everything I have is yours." [357]
Who says that? Who does that? What an incredibly amazing gift we have received.
He, the Creator of the heavens and the earth, He who brought light out of dark
and who brings warmth out of the chill has wrapped himself around us with eternal,
divine love. He persistently tells us that He wants us, that He loves us, that He
forgives us. His love is a perfect love, his mercy is a Divine Mercy. Even His most
cherished possession, His Divine Son, He gave to us! Embrace this gift!

It is easy to assume and to believe that we are unworthy of His gift, and perhaps
in our mind we indeed are not worthy. However, this is His gift that He gives. It is
our gift to receive. These sentiments of unworthiness that we often experience
were similarly felt by His closest disciples by His chosen few. To the anointed
leader of His Church, Simon Peter, who lacked belief in Christ's command for
him to go out fishing again into the Sea of Galilee at Lake Gennesaret, where he
was to again cast his net. Peter doubted and yet with the bounty received in his
fishing nets from the depths below, he expressed the natural inclination to persist
in his unworthiness before Him, "Depart from me, Lord, for I am a sinful man." [358]

Similarly for Paul, the amazing missionary of Christ's infant Church, who continually
questioned his worthiness before our Lord, "As to one born abnormally, He appeared
to me. For I am the least of the apostles, not fit to be called an apostle." [359] Feelings
of doubt, inadequacy and unworthiness are all too familiar for us all, but if and
when we accept His truth that He has chosen us, it is then that we are on the
path to salvation. It is then that we can begin to live according to His word and
His way. Jesus so clearly communicated His mission when He was questioned by
the Pharisees, "Those who are healthy do not need a physician, but the sick do.
I have not come to call the righteous to repentance but sinners." [360] He has come
for us all, He has come to each and every one of us, for we are all sinful. We must
open our hearts, our minds, our souls to Christ who is calling. Great things can

---

[357] Luke 15:31

[358] Luke 5:8

[359] 1 Corinthians 15:8-9

[360] Luke 5:31-32

be accomplished through Jesus Christ when we open ourselves to Him, when we fully trust in Him. We see this in Simon Peter who sank from the seas above in doubt, yet walked on the seas when he acted in faith and trust in Christ. His miraculous walking on the water was Christ's gift to His trusting disciple Peter.

This takes us back to our journey where we began herein and where we have learned that we must profess through our actions what Christ gave to us: "I am the way, and the truth, and the life. No one comes to the Father except through me." [361] We must do all that we can to model our actions and our behavior after the way that Christ taught us. We must seek truth and love. We must act with mercy and charity. We must not persist in a mindset of being the mighty and the lofty, but rather find solace in a mindset of the little and the lowly. Humbly we must continue to pick ourselves up and seek His way, His truth, His eternal life. This way is a continual battle between ups and downs, a struggle between good and evil. We must act in littleness to choose little ways to take the next step up and forward to Him. Each step is a step toward holiness and eternal unity with our Creator. His gift is there, awaiting us, we however must worthily receive it by uniting ourselves to His way.

We have focused on St. Thérèse the Little Flower's way of striving towards holiness via a sustained commitment to doing the small things, the lowly things, over and over again. Persistence though small little steps to receive His gift. This beautiful Saint taught us that we do not need to be great. We do not need to be known the world over for grandiose deeds. We can achieve sanctity, little sanctity, by committing ourselves to the persistent practice of little ways to holiness. We can do little, obscure deeds and grow in unity with Christ's way. We can make the "doing" of small, little deeds a part of who we are and how we interact with those around us. With our strand of deed beads in tow, we can use them to count the times and ways in which we practice holiness and in which we participate in the way of Christ. We can bring action and a commitment towards holiness if we bring to life the words of Dan Schutte in his hymn "Here I am, Lord" [362] when he writes: "I have heard you calling in the night, I will go Lord, if you lead me."

This slow and steady growth in sanctity is achieved through love, through persistence,

---

[361] John 14:6

[362] Dan Schutte. His Love is Holding You: Here I am, Lord, (1995).

through humility, through mercy. We have shown His light on the many ways in which He has taught us His way to holiness. In the preceding chapters, we focused on but 10 little ways to grow in unity with Christ. We considered ways in which we can elevate our commitment to communicating directly with Christ in prayer. It is here that we build depth to our relationship in Christ. We have discussed the need to remain strong in the face of the evil promptings of the devil. His sinister designs are unique for each and every individual, yet with Christ, we can overcome his temptations and rest in Christ's truth and peace. We have explored ways and times where we can grow in holiness by proactively unifying ourselves to the needs of others by a practice of charity and mercy. These were the ways of Christ and so too can they become our ways.

These *Little Ways to Little Sanctity* are frequently encountered during the passing of our days, seize them. Christ often spoke of the fact that it was the little children who were most aligned with His way and His life. He is speaking to our need to grow in littleness, to become humble in a world absorbed with itself. Further, we can accept the crosses we will encounter during our day, and willingly carry them as a sign of unity to the heavy millstone our Lord and Savior carried around His neck for the salvation of all mankind.

We can seek out and partake in the gifts Christ left us in this world of His, to help us on our road to salvation. These gifts are unique and readily available for us to embrace. Whether we spend time in a unifying love before our Lord in Adoration, or seek the intercession of His Mother whom He gave to the world, we are growing in holiness as we proactively make Christ a part of who we are and allow Him to align His divinity with the beating of our hearts. Jesus also left us all the beauty and treasures of His Holy Church. His beautiful Church has His word, His saints, His sacraments and so much more, all gifts to guide us on our journey. We also learned that Christ has called us to actively be a representation of His love, here on earth, to our neighbor in need. We must become ambassadors for Christ.

These are just but a few of the little ways to grow in little sanctity. St. Thérèse taught us each that we can use our deed beads to count the times and ways by which we make a steady commitment to a life in Christ, to a growth in holiness. Our deed beads can be an active tool to assist us in a persistent practice of focusing on the Way of Christ.

This daily practice and commitment to unifying our actions, our love and our souls to the Way and Life of Christ reminds me of a beautiful homily that was professed by the priest who celebrated the mass of my sister Kathy's wedding. Fr. Dennis stood before my sister and her husband-to-be and described the sacramental bond of unity they would now enter into and likened it to the braiding of two strands of rope to form one stronger more robust rope that is now there to lift both of them up and help propel them forward, together. These two braids, professed Fr. Dennis, were now one and could not be separated. This analogy helps describe our *Little Ways to Little Sanctity*. Imagine that each and every little way that we practice, each small gift completed out of love for our Lord, is a new small strand of thread that we weave around a broader strand that is Christ Himself. Each effort we undertake to more nearly align ourselves to the Ways of Christ is a unification of a new thread to the line of Christ. With each step in holiness, we lose an individual piece of ourselves, yet it transitions into the broader Body of Christ. With each gift of ourselves, we align ourselves to Christ's Will and we become a part of Christ our Savior. We become less separable and allow Him to become the more active mover in our lives. We tie ourselves to Christ in a more robust bond of unity and love. The two strands become braided together, not to be separated. Although Christ remains the anchor, we can slowly and steadily intertwine ourselves to our Master. This is our growth in holiness.

Saint Peter professed three very important concepts that unify the actions obtained through our "*Little Ways to Little Sanctity*" to the goal of an eternal life with Christ:

- "The God of all grace who called you to his eternal glory through Christ will himself restore, confirm, strengthen, and establish you after you have suffered a little." [363]

- "As he who called you is holy, be holy yourselves in every aspect of your conduct, for it is written, 'Be holy because I am holy'". [364]

- "Although you have not seen him you love him; even though you do not see him now yet believe in him, you rejoice with an indescribable and glorious joy, as you attain the goal of your faith, the salvation of your souls." [365]

---

[363] 1 Peter 5:10

[364] 1 Peter 1:15

[365] 1 Peter 1:8-9

Through our faith, through our Church, through the Gospels, we have glimpsed the Divinity of our Lord Jesus Christ. He is perfect holiness! Through His Blessed Mother, Mary, and in Joseph her most chaste spouse as well as in the Apostles, we have come to understand holiness in action. These mortal giants paved the way for so many saints who have come and gone over the centuries since Christ walked His Way. The Communion of Saints is made up of a beautiful contingent of holy souls, yet men and women who are not unlike each of us. However, they have chosen for Christ in a deep and meaningful way. They have acted in faith even with their inherent flaw of humanity. They have made the proactive decision to not sit idle and watch the tide of life pass by. Rather, they have embraced their faith, they have united themselves in countless different ways to the Way of our Savior, Jesus Christ. They have chosen Jesus and have then acted in alignment with their faith. The simplicity in their sanctity, although a difficult task to attain, lies in their choice to act in holiness. Our Heavenly Father has given us the freedom to make a choice for Him. We can make that choice! We can become saints by daily acts of faith in Christ. We can align ourselves to His Will and His Way by a slow, steady commitment to *Little Ways to Little Sanctity*.

Oh the joy if we are blessed to hear His voice:

> *"Well done, my good and faithful servant. Since you were faithful in small matters, I will give you great responsibilities. Come, share your master's joy."* [366]

---

[366] Matthew 25:23

Holy God, Holy Mighty One, Holy Immortal One,

Have Mercy on Me and on the Whole World

Holy God, Holy Mighty One, Holy Immortal One,

Have Mercy on Me and on the Whole World

Holy God, Holy Mighty One, Holy Immortal One,

Have Mercy on Me and on the Whole World.

"Jesus, I Trust in You"

. . . Amen

CPSIA information can be obtained
at www.ICGtesting.com
Printed in the USA
FSHW02n2208061018
52728FS